NEVER, NEVER, NEVER GIVE UP!

Kristen Dyson Maloney

NEVER, NEVER, NEVER GIVE UP!

An Inspirational IVF Story of Determination, Egg Donation and a Little Bit of Magic

Copyright © 2019 by Kristen Dyson Maloney

All Rights Reserved.

No part of this publication may be reproduced in any form or by any means, including photocopying, scanning, recording, or otherwise without prior written permission of the copyright holder.

www.nevergiveupbaby.com

ISBN: 978-0-6486812-0-5

NEVER, NEVER, NEVER GIVE UP!

An Inspirational IVF Story of Determination, Egg Donation and a Little Bit of Magic

Kristen Dyson Maloney

Dedication

For my brother – Mark Jason. Without you, this story may not be mine.

And for my step mum – Amanda, who gave our dreams life.

[1]
Jason Human

FOR AS LONG AS I can recall, I have been referred to as a miracle child by my parents—the one that defied all scientific odds to be here. My mum often shares the story of how she and my dad dreamed for a baby for many years before I came along. They had almost abandoned all hope of having children when an adoption agency contacted them advising that there was a two-year-old toddler in a Melbourne Babies Home that may be of interest to them. This particular child had "fallen through the Social Welfare cracks," but he was now potentially available for adoption. What a moment that must have been for them! They had been on a waiting list for a baby for several years, but even back then it was extraordinarily difficult to adopt in Australia, and so the odds were against them.

My parents promptly drove to Melbourne so full of excitement and anticipation, and upon arrival they were completely captivated by the beautiful, charismatic, little boy that was introduced to them. He took Mum's breath away. He appeared to be the only child, alone in a large dormitory full of cots, a situation which Mum found totally heartbreaking. They played with him, took him for a walk around the grounds of the institution, and then eagerly returned the following morning to spend more time with this adorable little boy who had already stolen their hearts. He was a total charmer, funny, witty and cute, and Mum and Dad were utterly enchanted. A few hours passed, and by then both of my parents were so won over that they asked if they could take him home to Bendigo for the weekend. Surprisingly, the nuns that ran the home hesitantly agreed. Even in the 70s this was not standard practice; however, Mum and Dad had excellent references. Also, they had been providing weekend respite to a mentally disabled child for several years, so they were already in the system on some level and were not viewed as complete strangers.

The little boy slotted right in at home immediately, and my parents were so enamoured by him that when Monday morning rolled around, they telephoned the nuns at the orphanage to advise that they wanted to adopt this delightful toddler and that they would prefer not to have to bring him back again, period! So just like that, my brother, Jason—or Mark, depending on who you ask—joined our family. You see, my parents already had a cat called Jason, and for reasons unbeknownst to me, Mum and Dad decided that they'd rather not rename the old cat. Instead they legally renamed the new child. My brother was named Mark Jason; however, Mark didn't stick, so from then on, they referred to the two Jasons as Jason Cat and Jason Human, and today my brother now answers to both names. He is Mark to most, but still Jason to his family.

About six months after Jay arrived, my mum fell pregnant naturally with me. You hear those kinds of stories frequently, but in my mum's case it was an incredible shock since years earlier she had been told by a gynaecologist that she had multiple rare problems that would make conception virtually impossible. Mum and Dad had a chemical incompatibility, and even more concerning was the fact that Mum was born with a double uterus and only one kidney. She was also 30 years old by that stage, which was considered positively ancient from a reproductive standpoint back then. So much so, that she would be medically categorised as a "geriatric" mother.

According to Mum, her gynaecologist was extremely concerned about the very high risk of miscarriage, along with the high possibility of physical or mental deformities. Despite this distressing information, Mum forged ahead and agreed to have a procedure which stitched me into the half of her uterus where I was growing at twelve weeks along. A premature birth was highly likely, and this was the 70s so there were no ultrasounds or 3D imagery available. Mum spent the entire pregnancy anxious and sick with worry about what the future may hold for her baby, and when I arrived just six weeks early, healthy and in perfect condition, she couldn't believe how lucky they were. And so, the story of the miracle child who had defied the odds was born.

I adored my brothers' story, but I didn't particularly like or appreciate mine. All that talk of fear and deformities was so unsettling. I much preferred hearing about the cute little boy that the nuns couldn't bear to part with, and who answered the door to his new extended family with such gusto just five minutes after arriving from the orphanage. My brother was the chosen one, a gift from the angels.

I spent my early adolescence harbouring a deep fear that I would struggle to have children just like my mum did. Call it intuition—or maybe my fear just stemmed from hers—but either way I distinctly recall sharing these concerns with my closest friends throughout my teens and scouring our school library for books on conception in the hope of learning more about infertility. I carried this angst like a monkey on my back throughout my 20s, but I hadn't yet met "the one" and I was willing to wait as long as it took to find him. Until then, my goal was to live in the moment as often as possible, and boy did I live. I bought my first house, I worked hard in my fulfilling career, I played hard on the weekends and I created countless memories with my beautiful friends. I built myself a full and fabulous life—a life that I was proud of.

[2]
Two Lost Souls Swimming in a Fishbowl

By the age of 32, I had spent several years in what could only be described as a highly dysfunctional relationship, and even back then, I think I knew it was destined to fail. I knew that this boyfriend was most likely not "the one" for me, but I was so entwined, so blindly loyal and so beholden to him, that I was finding it hard to break free. To me, he was a broken bird that needed rescuing, and I felt it was my duty to save him. I always see the best in people, and for some reason I felt that his intoxicatingly deep love for me made up for his mountain of misgivings. Sadly, in this case, I was being blinded by a charming fantasy, and it was to my detriment. This guy was a master manipulator, and everyone else could see it but me. I always found myself making excuses for him, and at the time I was convinced that the greatest loves were also the most painful. Looking back, I endured more pain than could ever be considered acceptable. I'm not sure why I put up with so little from him for so long, but my expectations continually lowered in line with his piteous efforts, until I finally ran out of excuses.

The catalyst for me was when he failed to attend one of my best friends' wedding in Bali. Stacey (the beautiful bride) had been like a sister to me since the age of 13, and my boyfriend had promised he would meet me in Bali prior to the big day. When he called me on the day before the wedding with a ridiculous excuse as to why he was no longer coming, I was totally devastated. It was the last straw, the final brick in a wall that had been building for years, and I finally woke up and saw him for who he really was: a narcissistic liar. And just like that, I was done. I switched off from him, and the 100kg monkey on my back just instantly disappeared. I'd been carrying a dead weight for far too long, and that experience of releasing myself of something so toxic and gripping was surprisingly effortless and liberating. I felt relief, I felt like myself again, and I felt free.

That night in Bali, I reconnected with one of my oldest friends, Richard Maloney. We had been extremely close growing up, but we had drifted apart in more recent years due to distance. We originally met at kindergarten at the ripe old age of three, and we reacquainted on the school bus at fifteen. He was a total rebel sitting on the back seat of the bus, and he exuded a confidence that left me in awe. From that day on, Rich quickly became one of the most consistent people in my life, and we ran in the same close circle throughout our teens and twenties. When I was 19, my mum (now amicably divorced from my father) suddenly announced that she was moving to Port Macquarie with her new husband. Being so unexpectedly and abruptly excused from the nest felt almost apocalyptic at the time, and I was at a complete loss on where to live, so I decided to move to Queensland for what I hoped would be a fresh start and a new adventure. It was such a difficult and confusing period in my life, and when the two friends I had moved to Queensland with both returned to Melbourne within a few short months, I felt incredibly lost. I was broke, completely alone and now seriously contemplating moving back home with my tail between my legs, and then along came Richard.

After a quick visit to the Gold Coast to see my new world, Rich decided to move up from Melbourne to Queensland too. He hitched a ride on the back of the removalist truck that was delivering my furniture, and he moved in around the corner. We were two lost souls seeking something bigger than we could explain or understand, and Rich provided the familial reassurance I needed to stay.

Our connection was kindred on many levels, and we became so close in our time up there that I even asked Rich to give my 21st birthday speech, which he delivered beautifully. We shared a fascination for the realm of metaphysics, and we would spend hours discussing our spiritual endeavours, each on our own personal quest for the ultimate meaning of life. We had a deep and unique bond based on shared ideologies unlike anything I had ever established with anyone, but in spite of our chemistry, for the most part, we remained platonic. I think during those years on the Gold Coast, I needed Richard's companionship above all else. Our friendship was far too important to risk by taking things to the next level.

Three years into our shared adventure, Rich moved on to travel Australia playing professional football for a few years, followed by a move to Perth for seven years to captain an elite football team. We maintained our bond via lengthy telephone calls during this period, but we very rarely saw each other, with geography and other relationships always keeping us apart.

When we finally caught up at our dear friend Stacey's magical wedding in Bali, something major had shifted between us. It was confusing at first, but also undeniably powerful. We both felt this formidable explosion of emotions at exactly the same time, something I now look back on as fateful. By day two of the trip, we were secretly holding hands, playing it coy in public while we attempted to get our heads around what was happening between us. Our relationship progressed quickly, and Rich extended his trip in Bali to stay with me. I couldn't believe how easy it was—he made me feel like sunshine, and with him I had always felt like the best version of myself. We fell madly for each other on that trip, and it was instant or had slowly progressed over a lifetime, depending on how you viewed it. How funny that my soul mate had been right in front of me throughout my entire life. The universe is serendipitous like that. It's simply amazing.

After just a few months together, Rich moved in with me, and six months after that he proposed. It was such a thrilling, exciting time, though for me it was slightly tainted by my underlying fears of infertility. I was so anxious about my ability to procreate that I decided to take the bull by the horns and see a fertility specialist. I couldn't help but wonder whether Rich would still want to marry me if I couldn't have children, and more than anything I was seeking peace of mind. I was referred to a local specialist who conducted a myriad of tests, and I was beyond delighted when he declared me to be very fertile indeed. It was one of the greatest moments of relief I can ever recall, and with my deepest fears now allayed, I could relax, be young, have fun and enjoy being engaged without racing into parenthood. And my god did we have fun! Such a blissful, free and easy time in our lives. I had never felt so happy, so supported or so fulfilled.

We married upstairs at the iconic Stokehouse restaurant on the beach in St. Kilda, and our day was utter perfection on every level. Even the heavy rain (which in so many cultures represents unity, renewal, cleansing and fertility) just added to the theatre and the joy of the day. After our wedding, we felt we were ready for a baby immediately. Many of my closest friends already had children, and at 34 I felt like my biological clock was seriously ticking. About six months later I fell pregnant, and I was absolutely elated. I remember thinking how lucky I was to be avoiding the stress and pain of infertility. This feeling was only intensified by the fact that we had several dear friends going through IVF at the time. I so vividly remember the night I celebrated my 35th birthday with Rich and all our closest friends. I felt so special, so gifted and so proud to be pregnant. We announced our pregnancy to the world that night despite me being only seven weeks along. It was just too exciting not to share.

Being pregnant was all-consuming but in the very, very best way. I felt like the cat that got the cream, and I loved knowing I had this special little secret that had only been shared with those closest to us. The following week at work my bliss continued until I started to feel a few unnerving tummy twinges and I discovered I was spotting. The fear and sense of dread a woman experiences when this happens in pregnancy is indescribable; however, sadly, far too many of us know that feeling all too well. I called my doctor and I was booked in for an urgent scan that afternoon. And just like that, I lost a large piece of my innocence. The scan confirmed my greatest fear: that our little baby was gone. The embryo had stopped growing at seven weeks, and I felt like I had literally lost a living, breathing child. For the first time in my life, I felt utterly and irreparably broken, and the prolonged and intense physical pain that followed that night as I miscarried only exacerbated my mental anguish.

I never did conceive naturally again after that loss. We tried everything. Acupuncture, fertility diets, Clomid, a laparoscopy, every supplement, Chinese herb and gimmick on the market, I even stood on my head—nothing worked. And so, by my 36th birthday, we were reluctantly moving on to IVF. I couldn't believe I was in this position after conceiving quite easily that first time, but I believed with every inch of my soul that IVF would be the holy grail of answers for us. I was sure we would succeed first try and that all would be right in the world once I was holding my baby. I was still so naive and unaffected at that point, but my starry-eyed outlook was to be very short-lived.

[3]
And so it begins...

June 2012

When we finally commenced our first round of IVF, I had fully regained the spring in my step. It felt redemptive and cathartic to be taking the control back. I had researched fanatically for months in preparation, feeling mentally steadfast and so resolute that I would sail through this process. I was positive that we would be part of the lucky 30% where IVF works FIRST TIME, and I was just so ready to win! We had been told that there was no medical reason why we couldn't get pregnant, which was extremely reassuring. Richard had been tested, and we were told he had "super sperm," and I was totally fine, so nobody was going to warn me that the outcome of this first cycle could be anything less than a home run.

I had no questions for my doctor (the same one that had told me my fertility looked great a few years back). I felt I already knew everything. I had already been taken on the IVF journey by Stacey, who was at that time in the middle of her fourth round. I knew every excruciating detail about the injections, the hormones, the procedures, and of course, the devastating disappointment one experiences when it's unsuccessful. I was with her on her journey every step of the way, and I distinctly recall that first bitter phone call on Christmas Eve when she announced that her first IVF cycle had failed. I literally started sobbing in the street. My heart broke for them with all that they had already endured, and I just couldn't bring myself to consider the possibility of having to deal with that deep and profound sense of loss personally.

And so, we embarked on our first IVF expedition of injections, stimulating hormones, blood tests and a sea of exploding emotions. On around the seventh day, I eagerly went in for an ultrasound to see just how many eggs my body was going to produce for harvest. I was excited, optimistic and a little nervous—so much was riding on this. In the car on the way to the clinic I started to daydream. Ideally, we would get 15-20 eggs. That way we should see a minimum of eight fertilised and at least five make it to day five blastocysts. We would have one for transfer and four to put on ice. Perfecto! That seemed to be a reasonable and very achievable goal.

I hadn't felt the need to bring Rich along to this appointment. I was simply ticking another box in the process and I didn't think this step was overly important. This was the easy and rewarding part, or so I thought. When the sonographer started looking concerned and searching my uterus for my 15-20 follicles and the ultrasound screen looked pretty damn vacant, to say I was ill prepared was an understatement. A familiar and foreboding feeling washed over me. Here I was again, lying on an ultrasound table, desperately searching for something that just didn't appear to be there. Last time it was a heartbeat, this time it was the initial seeds of life required just to take that first step towards achieving a heartbeat. The words that followed are etched in my soul and continued to haunt me for years. "Does early menopause run in your family Kristen"? Ahhhhhhh, excuse me? What the FUCK? What THE ACTUAL FUCK? I was floored. Shocked. Broken all over again. "No" I heard myself saying. "That's impossible, I'm only 36".

The days that ensued were an emotional blur, but I do remember feeling defiant, and just so certain that they must have this all wrong. That first IVF cycle was abruptly cancelled. There is, of course, no point in having your eggs surgically harvested when you only have one follicle. Women release one egg each month without IVF, so it would have been a futile process. My body just hadn't responded at all, so we needed to up the ante.

The grand plan in the month that followed was basically a last-ditch Hail Mary. I would be injecting the strongest dose of stimulating hormone legally permitted in Australia in order to inspire my body to respond, hopefully bringing a few follicles back from the dead in the process. It was the best and only shot we had—they were going to pump me so full of drugs that my few remaining eggs would hopefully have no choice but to surface.

We were relieved and cautiously optimistic after the first ultrasound in that cycle. I had eight follicles. How dare they suggest early menopause. Early menopause my ass! I went in for my first IVF-egg-retrieval surgery with renewed optimism, and I was told we could probably expect four mature eggs. A very low number in the IVF world, but three more than last month, so we were making progress. Unlike most people who dread surgery, I must admit I quite like it. Maybe it's the attention you receive, or the warm and fuzzy drugs they give you. Maybe it's the recovery process, where for a short while everything you need to be responsible for in life is taken care of by someone else. Whatever the reason, I went in feeling fearless, excited and so ready to get this baby show on the road. When I awoke from the procedure, my doctor came by and told me that they had managed to extract five mature eggs. I was so thrilled and just so incredibly relieved. We even got a bonus egg! Now they just had to fertilise those five eggs with Richard's sperm, allow them to develop to day five, choose the best embryo, transfer it to me, and voila, I'd be pregnant. Too easy! I was sent on my way and told that the embryologists would contact me the following day to let us know how many eggs fertilised. I went home, drank a glass or two of red (please don't judge, I'd done my part and I was certain I was about to abstain for nine months) and I revelled in feelings of achievement, peace and satisfaction.

The following morning, we received the call, and I wish I could say it was great news. I was quickly learning that in the IVF world, things rarely go to plan. Two of the eggs had literally shattered when they attempted to fertilise them, which is a sure indication of very poor quality. One egg had fertilised but then failed to develop overnight, and so now only two embryos remained. In light of this, my doctor required me to come in for a day three transfer. Day three transfers are quite unusual nowadays and are only necessary when there is a very low number of embryos or when the embryo quality is poor. All clinics now recommend a day-five transfer, since many embryos arrest on day three. By observing them for an additional two days, they can identify those that are of sound quality. In my case, though, we had neither the numbers nor the quality, so day three it would be. Fuck.

I distinctly remember the day of the transfer, and overall it was a pretty disheartening experience. I had frantically googled day and night in the lead-up, chasing hope and searching for any stories of success from a day three transfer. Unfortunately, the overwhelming majority of the stories I had read had not resulted in success, so by the time we reached the hospital I was feeling dejected and pessimistic, while also suffering from a severe hormone hangover. Nonetheless, I kept telling myself to buck up, that there was still a chance, miracles do happen, etc. Today I would be pregnant until proven otherwise.

Back then, my IVF clinic required patients to have a very full bladder during transfer, so by the time we went in to prepare for the procedure, I was already feeling hideous with a near exploding bladder. We were advised by our nurse that the quality of our two embryos had been graded as B and C, and it was only day three. Fuck again. A five-day-old grade A embryo is what is most likely to result in a successful pregnancy, so we were already feeling deflated when the doctor unexpectedly suggested we transfer both embryos. At that point, I knew we were probably screwed.

It's against protocol in Australia to transfer more than one embryo unless the quality is low and there is no hope of freezing. So, there I sat, confused and half-naked in a sterile, clinical white room the size of a wardrobe, with an impassive, expressionless doctor who would not even look me in the eye. Not even once. I just wanted some sort of reassurance or encouragement from him, but I received neither. Even my valid and obvious questions were awkwardly evaded. He just didn't provide any straight answers.

In that moment, I sensed that my doctor was in the lucrative business of IVF first and foremost and that I was just a number to him. I knew that in his scientific mind, these two little embryos were probably not going to become our babies, but I also knew that I'd do anything and everything in my power to defy the odds and provide them their best chance at life. I could absolutely be the exception, and almost anything is possible.

[4]
The cold, hard facts...

July 2012

After the transfer, I was reluctant to get up and off the table in case the embryos fell out. I was also terrified to pee in case I peed the embryos out. Both concerns were superseded, however, by my overwhelming desire (driven by excruciating bladder pain) to get up and urinate. An almost overflowing bladder has got to be a form of torture somewhere.

Rich had to get on a plane to London that night for work, so my mum (now happily living the retiree dream with her husband, George, in Port Macquarie) came down to stay with me for moral support. She probably hadn't bargained on waiting on me hand and foot, but such was my desire to make this work that I insisted on going to bed for the weekend—only getting up to sparingly use the bathroom. There may not have been any science backing my idea that bed rest would improve my chances of pregnancy, but to me it just made sense. Gravity, right? Never mind that every woman who conceives naturally gets on with life after doing the deed. I was determined to have no regrets. I also ate pineapple and drank raspberry tea (having read that these may also help) and I desperately prayed to God for the first time in my adult life.

After that weekend, I went back to work and tried ineffectively to get through the remaining five days before my blood test without wondering whether I was pregnant every 60 seconds of the day. I failed dismally, and those thoughts engulfed every inch of my being for every waking moment of every day, my only reprieve being sleep. On day seven (a Friday), I took the blood test on my way to work, and then waited impatiently all day for the call. I was almost hyperventilating when it finally came as I drove home from work. I tried to visualise my nurse, Louise, saying, "Kristen, congratulations, you're pregnant", but deep in my heart I'm sure I already knew that was likely not happening. And as I held my breath as she delivered the news, I remember thinking how hard it must be for her to continually break women's hearts with those two agonising, desolating words, "I'm sorry".

And so again my heart felt irreparably broken, and in that moment the pain cut me so deeply that it was physical. I went home and howled in my mum's arms, feeling betrayed by the world, and God and my faulty, washed-up body. And then after about one hour of sobbing and wallowing in self-pity, I somehow flicked my inner stonewall switch and I bucked up. Looking back, I'm not completely sure how I did that, but emotional pain was no stranger to me, so perhaps it was a coping mechanism that I had slowly evolved with every heartbreak I'd been dealt throughout my life. I defiantly decided to text my friends letting them know that this would not break me, and Mum and I played happy songs and drank white wine. This time I felt stronger and more resilient like I was subconsciously prepared for the sense of loss. It still hurt, but not for as long and not as deeply as last time. I was able to just push through it. There was more than one way to build a family, and if we couldn't do it this way then there were so many other avenues to explore. I felt hopeful again, and probably deep down relieved that that whole heart-wrenching experience was over.

I also now understood why IVF can break you, and why so many women give up and walk away empty-handed. There is no emotional toll quite like it, I'm sure. It's so brutal when it fails. The pain hits you like a fierce punch in the face, and if you've ever been viciously punched, you will understand why so many don't go back. The anticipation is even worse than the punch itself, however—way worse, I think. Sometimes it's better to know than not to know, regardless of the outcome. IVF is a horrific concoction of pre-emptive pain and fear, mixed in with the purest and most blissful sense of optimism and hope that you know will likely be cruelly ripped away in an instant. It's a full body blow, with an aftermath that can leave you scarred forever.

The following week I returned to my doctor ready to hear all about the shiny new plan. I was no longer a fan of his, but I needed to keep the ball rolling, and I was ready to leap back in and take the next step in our journey since the last step had failed so dismally. I was astonished, almost beyond words, when the shiny new grand plan turned out to be exactly the SAME as the shitty old plan that hadn't worked the first time and almost broke me in the process. Sorry but am I missing something? I thought. Isn't that old plan precisely the one we should now be avoiding since it didn't even come close to working? Right there and then I received my silver bullet, and I knew that this guy would not be my guy anymore. There had been so many red flags along the way with him. Exhibit A was the fact that Richard thought he was an arrogant asshole from day one. In all our meetings he had never even acknowledged Rich, never spoken to him, never shook his hand, never even looked at him. He had already planted so many seeds of doubt in my mind, and my intuition had been screaming "move on" from the beginning. So why was I still here?

Unfortunately, my despairing need for a baby had always screamed louder, but now it was irrefutable and I had received clear and undeniable validation. I'd done my homework, obsessively. There were so many alternative protocols available to poor responders like me, and yet, here he was not even pretending to be exploratory or creative? This was an aha moment for me, such is the juggernaut that is the IVF industry. A booming sales commodity with insanely lucrative growth prospects that preys on the vulnerable. There will always be those medical professionals who succumb to the woo of the cash and would rather peddle a few rounds of snake oil before stepping things up to provide meaningful odds.

Intuitively and pre-emptively, I had already made an appointment for a second opinion with another doctor. I knew Stacey and several other friends had achieved success with a renowned IVF doctor called Lynn Burmeister. She was considered one of the best but I wanted someone closer to home, and my acupuncturist knew of a doctor that was considered to be a trailblazer much like Lynn. She said he was the guy you go to when you've gone as far as you can go with everyone else. I called him my 'last chance saloon' guy. His name was Dr Nick Lolatgis, and he could not have been more different than his predecessor.

The first time I met Dr Nick, I was immediately impressed by his bedside manner (or lack thereof). He did not mince words, and he cut straight to the chase. So refreshing! I felt I'd already been fed enough bullshit to last a lifetime, and I was eager to hear the cold, hard facts, however painful. Dr Nick had access to my history, as he worked under the same IVF banner as my previous doctor. He had also requested that I have every test available prior to our meeting to ensure we didn't waste any more time. I went in with an idea of what he would say, and my ideas were corroborated. Dr Nick said that I had an AMH (egg supply) of three. An abysmal and almost undetectable level. He said that even at my age, egg quality and quantity often go hand in hand, and to add insult to injury, I had an overabundance of natural killer cells, resulting in a form of immunological infertility. In a nutshell, I was a very poor candidate for conventional IVF, and even if he "threw the kitchen sink at me" with optimising treatments, at best, our odds would only be 5% per cycle.

Then came the game changer I'd been waiting for.

Dr Nick had a growing number of clients who were opting to use egg donors. Donors from Australia, USA, India, South Africa and Greece. Nick was Greek, and he said he had a partnership over there and that he had "eggs on tap" in Greece. Eggs on tap, how amazing! Using donor eggs with the right accompanying treatments would increase our chances from 5% to around 75%

per transfer. I really liked those odds, and surprisingly I felt nothing but excitement. I had already mourned my crappy old eggs after the last cycle, and deep down I knew my last doctor had offered me false hope. To me this was a no brainer, and one I had already been investigating in spades. We agreed that I would discuss it with Rich and that I could contact Dr Nick's office to be put in touch with some of the past patients that had used international egg donors to figure out what destination could work best for us.

Before I left Dr Nick's office, I asked him about why things may have gone south so quickly for me when in 2009 all of my fertility levels were so good. After a quick look at his screen, he said, "Darling, your fertility was already very poor back then. When you were tested three years ago, your AMH was only 7 when it should have been between 15 and 30". I was dumbfounded. This was the biggest, hardest body blow thus far. I felt cheated beyond words, and I desperately needed answers. How the fuck did I not know about this in 2009? My world just kept on being rocked, but not in the good way. What else could the universe throw at me?

[5]
Dr. Disappointment

THAT NIGHT, I was like a woman possessed, and I drafted and sent the following letter via email to my old doctor:

12/8/12

Dear Tom*,

I wanted to write this letter to express my extreme disappointment and confusion relating to your handling of my infertility.

It has been brought to my attention that my AMH levels measured at around seven (pmol/L) when I came to you to have my fertility assessed in 2009. This was the sole reason for my visit to you in 2009, and at that time I was told by you that my fertility "looked good".

Because of your positive assurance, my husband and I delayed our plans to start a family and did not seek *further evaluation until 2011. Even at that time, you never mentioned my poor AMH results, and so we continued a slow road which eventually led us to IVF in June 2012.*

You can imagine our shock when our IVF was cancelled, and we were told that I was a poor responder and that I may be on the way to 'early menopause'. It didn't add up, and so I asked questions relating to the tests that were conducted in 2009. Again, I was told that at that time everything had come back as normal by you.

I then insisted on a second AMH test, which you stated would be a waste of time since the result would not influence the protocol you would be prescribing for my second IVF attempt. I had the test done despite this recommendation, and I was told by Louise that I would be notified as soon as the results came in. I enquired about these results on two occasions, and on both occasions, I was told that the results had not yet come back.

It was only through seeking a second opinion from another IVF specialist last week that I was informed of my extremely poor AMH results from both 2009 (just seven) and 2012 (now just three). I am now on the verge of falling into the very low/undetectable fertility range.

Ovarian Fertility Potential	pmol/L	ng/mL
Optimal Fertility	28.6 - 48.5	4.0 - 6.8
Satisfactory Fertility	15.7 - 28.6	2.2 - 4.0

Low Fertility	2.2 - 15.7	0.3 - 2.2
Very Low / undetectable	0.0 - 2.2	0.0 - 0.3
High Level	> 48.5	> 6.8

This is extremely confusing to me, and I'm devastated to learn of this misdiagnosis on your behalf in 2009, followed by your poor handling of my situation from our commencement of IVF in 2012. At the very least, if results were inconclusive, surely you could have conducted more tests?

I am now faced with the possibility of never conceiving, and had I known in 2009 what I know now, we would have taken immediate and aggressive action, rather than waiting. I had 100% faith in you as my doctor, so much so that I have referred many friends on to you.

I would appreciate a written response at your earliest convenience.

Kind regards,

Kristen Dyson
*Doctor's actual name not disclosed.

While writing that letter was somewhat cathartic, I had no intention of letting this go in that moment. I had been wronged and robbed of the most precious thing that I could never get back in this journey: time. I felt betrayed and scorned by someone I had paid to help me, and I needed to know why he had failed me so spectacularly.

When I received a bumbling phone call from Tom the following day, I was not at all surprised. I knew he wouldn't respond in writing. He had messed up and he wasn't about to deliver me an opportunity to sue on a silver platter. The phone call was pathetic. At no point did he apologise (that may have also opened him up to being sued) and at no point did he admit any wrongdoing. He gave me a spiel about the AMH test being unreliable (though it is widely recognised as the MOST accurate and reliable indicator of a woman's ovarian reserve) and he stuttered and muttered throughout the call, failing to provide any justifiable reasoning for his gross omission. I was stunned by his lack of empathy, and overall, I just felt saddened by yet another sense of loss. I took no further action, despite being urged to by my loved ones. It wasn't the time to seek vengeance. I had work to do, and I knew there was a little soul out there in the universe just waiting for the opportunity to join our family. This is where I needed to remain invested. And I was confident Tom would now take more care with his future patients.

The weeks that followed were a frenetic blur. Any spare time I had outside of work was spent searching the internet. First, we had to decide which country to choose for our egg donor, and once narrowed down, we had to decide on a clinic within our chosen country. You may be wondering why we weren't looking in our own back yard first. This is complicated. In Australia, there are many rules attached to egg donation. It must be completely altruistic, meaning you cannot compensate the donor for their time. Anonymity is not an option. The donor must have already completed their family and the donor should be aged 23-33, thus ruling out all of my close friends and female cousins. At the time, if you wanted to find an egg donor in Australia, you had to either know someone or place an ad online or in a newspaper, alongside ads placed by so many other desperate people longing for a child of their own. For every woman out there looking to donate her eggs, there were probably 100 ads pleading for eggs. I didn't like my chances, and the whole idea of it made me uncomfortable. It was like the women seeking a donor were trying to outdo each other in terms of whose story was the saddest and most desperate. Also, at the time I was quite attracted to the idea of partial anonymity. I wanted my child to know something about the genetic history and the donor herself (photographs, personal details, family health report, psychological evaluation etc) without having to have her in our lives. I feel differently about that now, but at the time I thought that was the best option for our family. It was for this reason that we narrowed it down to two countries: South Africa or USA. They were the only countries offering a choice of donor with accompanying background information. All the other countries on offer required complete anonymity, meaning you had no idea who your donor was, what she looked like, or where she came from. Just totally random. I felt I had already relinquished so much control on this journey, and the idea of that was just too much for me. I at least wanted to choose someone that looked a little like me, and more importantly, I wanted my child to know something about their genetic background when they had questions in the future.

I had initiated discussions with what I thought to be the best clinics on offer in each country. One clinic was in Cape Town South Africa, and the other in San Diego California. Both had extremely high success rates nearing 80%; however, the one that really appealed to me was San Diego, because they offered a unique success guarantee program. Basically, you pay them one set upfront fee and you keep doing IVF cycles until you achieve a live birth. If you haven't achieved success after all embryos (both fresh and frozen) are transferred, you receive a full refund. The cost was four times the cost of one transfer cycle in Cape Town, but here I would be guaranteed a baby. I could potentially go to Cape Town four times and still have nothing to show for it. At least in San Diego I would get my money back if it didn't work. I also really liked the principle of a mutual commitment. It felt right and it made sense to me. I mean, clearly they would go to greater lengths than usual to ensure my success if they had skin in the game. San Diego was by far the most appealing option to both of us. Just one teensy little problem. Where in god's name were we going to find $40,000?

# [6]

What country, what country?

IN THE WEEKS THAT followed, I continued communicating and exploring options with both Cape Town and San Diego. I was granted access to their exclusive in-house donor programs, and we were able to view the profiles of their many registered egg donors. Regrettably for us, the South African egg donor laws prevented them from providing detailed information on their donors, as donation is strictly anonymous and only early childhood photos (often of poor quality) are provided. In the state of California, however, the donor laws are considered the most relaxed in the world. Donation may be anonymous or open (depending on the wishes of the donor) and we were able to view many recent photographs, along with detailed genetic, psychological and personal details, dating back three generations. This meant so much to me, and a lack of donor transparency was the only reason we had excluded all other countries. South Africa as a destination also made me quite nervous.

While Cape Town is a developed city, it is second world, lacking in stability and safety in comparison to Australia, and with a notorious reputation for violent crime. Add that to the fact that it is over 20 hours travel away, and San Diego was now looking extremely appealing.

Still, we had to overcome the glaring and blatant issue of money, or lack thereof. We had been struggling financially for some time at this point. Rich and I love to take risks in life, and so in the final months leading up to our wedding, Rich quit his job to start his own business—straight after we had purchased our first property together. The worst house in the best street, demolition worthy, but perfect for its intent, which was a dual townhouse development. When we confessed to the loan manager at the bank about our change in financial circumstances prior to settlement, he put his hands over his ears and declared that he hadn't heard any of what we'd just said. We thought we were doing the right thing by being honest, but clearly our loan could not have legally proceeded had our loan manager not chosen to look the other way. We were about to get in way over our heads, but at this point we had no idea. We sincerely believed Rich would be earning big money in the first few years of operation. This was so not the case, and our IVF endeavours thus far, coupled with the investment required to build a new business, had already put a huge dent in our credit cards. Those that say money doesn't make you happy seriously must have money! These were dark days for us, but thankfully we were unaware of the fact that it was going to get so much worse.

At no point throughout our baby journey did I allow money to impact on our broader decisions though. I had an investment property I'd purchased ten years prior that I was very prepared to sell, and I think we would have sold our house too had it been necessary. You can't put a price on family, but it sometimes comes down to how far you are prepared to go. For us, we were prepared to go all the way baby, whatever the cost financially, physically, emotionally and spiritually. I had Richard's full backing and at no point did he ever entertain or suggest the possibility of giving up. I will never forget his unconditional and limitless support. Many men would have wavered, especially when it came to using an egg from a stranger. He never made me feel broken or "less than" for needing a donor. On the contrary, he was the one that kept reminding me that biology truly didn't matter. This was in spite of the fact that several of our closest friends had been very vocal about the fact that they would NEVER go down the donor path and that they would sooner just go without children. I think some people are just really hung up on their own genetics, and while I respect that, it's so not us.

So, as we continued to go backwards financially, we also continued to explore plausible ways to get the money we needed to proceed with San Diego - It wasn't just the 40K for the success guarantee program that we needed. It was also the cost of the donor (5K), the travel, accommodation, drugs (for myself and the donor), and Dr Nick's fees here. All up 60K for our first trip, so we absolutely needed to sell my apartment, and we needed to do it fast. I started to make the necessary arrangements, first setting up an evaluation meeting and then investigating how much notice I needed to give my tenant. Sixty days' notice felt like a lifetime. Add time for repairs, a sales campaign, auction and settlement, and we were looking at a minimum of six months. I felt frustrated, impatient and beaten down. And then, something wonderful and unforgettable happened.

I was over at my dad and his wife's house, when my stepmum, Amanda, came into the room and declared that she had an announcement to make. The moments that followed will be etched in my brain for life. She very calmly proclaimed, "You're going to San Diego and we're going to pay for it. It's not a loan, it's an investment, in our grandchildren." I was stunned, lost for words, and I just started sobbing uncontrollably as though I'd just been told we had won the lottery. It was a rarely experienced moment of perfection in life, a moment where the weight of the world instantly melted from my shoulders. The feelings of relief, immense gratitude, excitement and hope were overwhelming, and I wept for one thousand reasons. It was the most remarkably generous gesture anyone has ever offered us, at the exact time when we needed it most. Amanda had always been a bit like a guardian angel in our lives, picking up the "mum" slack after my own mum decided to leave Melbourne while I was still in my teens, but this was so next level, and also the world's most over-the-top gift. If this worked, my children would always be reminded that they would not be here had it not been for Amanda. And Dad, of course, but Amanda first and foremost. She was the one driving this extraordinary gift.

It felt incredible to have the costs of the guarantee program covered by my parents. Such a pressure released. They covered the costs of all of the drugs too, leaving us to cover the costs of the donor and our travel. Totally achievable with a modest redraw from our home loan. In addition, I worked for Qantas Loyalty as an account manager, so our flights cost next to nothing. I had first-class clearance too, so providing there were seats available on the day, we could fly first-class direct to LA. I could literally feel the winds of change around me, and it felt divine. We selected a beautiful donor who had never donated her eggs before but already had her own child, so we considered her the perfect candidate. The next step was to get our cycles and bodies in sync and to book in all of my appointments here in Melbourne. It's actually not so easy to get your body in sync with another human being, and when they're on the other side of the world attending a different medical clinic, that adds yet another layer of complexity. There are so many variables and so much that can go wrong. I had to start taking and building on my medication at the exact USA time specified and ensure I accurately accounted for time differences. I needed to start progesterone injections at the precise moment specified (even if it was mid-flight). I had to ensure my "oven" was ready and that my uterine lining was thick and fluffy and ready to embrace an embryo. I had scans and blood tests here in Melbourne to check that everything was progressing well, and I then had to rely on the nurses here to communicate my results with San Diego. At any moment the cycle could be cancelled due to the donor or I not progressing optimally, and with every day that passed, my nerves became more frayed.

To add to my worries, we were flying standby on my Qantas staff-travel entitlement. We had never done this before, so we just hoped there would be seats remaining on the A380 to LA. It's a monster aeroplane that seats 544, and in the days leading up to our travel we could log in and see that there were still plenty of seats available, so we were confident.

There was, however, always that risk that we wouldn't get on, and for Rich it was a non-negotiable. He couldn't miss that flight. He had a donation to make in San Diego and it had to coincide perfectly with our donor's egg retrieval. Yet again the timing was everything, and without Richard's sperm it would all have been in vain.

[7]
Up, Up and Away

December 2012

The night before we were due to fly out, we watched the staff-travel website like hawks. There were Qantas flights leaving from Melbourne, Sydney and Brisbane direct to LA that following morning, so we figured worst case we could fly to Sydney or Brisbane on the first flight out and still make the LA flight in plenty of time. We set the alarm and checked how many seats remained every three hours. You wouldn't believe how many people book international trips last minute! The available seats dwindled, but a Melbourne departure was still our best bet, so we headed to the airport hoping and praying for a seat. Our main goal was to get on the plane, with the cherry being a first-class or business-class seat. When we got to the check-in, we were advised that there were no business seats left, so it was economy or first. There were three economy seats left, two first-class seats and ten staff listed. Shit. Very average odds. We were instructed to come back 30 minutes prior to boarding time, and so we went to a café—for me to hyperventilate and for Rich to strategise.

I was in a particularly vulnerable and edgy state at this point, having been pumped full of hormones and steroids to prevent my body from rejecting a pregnancy. I was fearful, anxious and unable to think clearly or exercise anything resembling logic. I knew I was verging on a full-blown panic attack when Rich suggested he just buy an Air New Zealand seat. We only needed to get him there urgently, whereas I could always fly the next day if we missed out. The ticket was cheaper than a full Qantas airfare, but still insanely expensive given we would be booking at the airport on the day of departure. As our very frugal family financier, I couldn't quite bear the thought of spending thousands on a seat that we may still get almost free, so we agreed to wait until the very last moment, with the Air New Zealand flight departing just 30 minutes after the Qantas flight. When the time came to return to the Qantas desk, there were eight other staff impatiently standing there with their luggage, all of us vying for those last five seats. That was, of course, assuming no one had booked a seat in the last two hours, in which case there would be even less of a chance of getting a seat. It was so down to the wire that when the customer service lady came out from behind the Qantas desk, Rich was already standing by Air New Zealand with his ticket seconds from being purchased. She reeled off three names from one family—they each got a boarding pass, and then I heard "Kristen Dyson and Richard Maloney". She handed me the boarding passes and they were both first-class seats. Noooooooo freakinggggggggg wayyyyyyyy! I was shocked and, of course, utterly elated. Rich (who had been waiting on the other end of the phone while standing by at Air New Zealand) let out a massive "yeeehahhh" and came running back over.

There was no time to waste so we were issued with EXPRESS Passes and we started sprinting towards customs. As we were running, a guy who had been waiting near me in the staff huddle approached us, grabbed Richard's arm and aggressively demanded to know, "What ranking are you"? Qantas staff standby seats are prioritised according to the ranking of your position within the company, and usually only the most senior executives qualify as being "upgradable to first". As an account manager, I'm not sure why I fell into that category, my role wasn't senior, but it was completely legitimate. It was a point of contention for some Qantas staff, as they rightly felt that the ranking system was unfair and illogical. One of Richard's best mates is an international pilot and was still ineligible for the same benefits that I was. He had every right to think that was unjust. On that day, though, my high ranking saved us, and I was so grateful for it. I was probably the only staff member there eligible for those first-class seats, and this guy was really pissed. Rich shrugged him off and kept running, ignoring the angry shouts behind us. I felt his pain. He and his wife were probably heading off on a dream holiday, but at the same time that's what happens in life when you roll the dice. You win some, you lose some. Right now, we were winning, but still, such a long and bumpy road lay ahead.

Once we were onboard, we were escorted to the front of the plane by the most charming, warm and incredibly camp flight attendant (and aren't they just the best kind)! The relief and happiness I felt was overwhelming. I couldn't hold the tears of joy back, and so I sat in my very fancy first-class compartment sipping French champagne and marvelling at how far we'd come and how close we now were to being parents. Finally, it seemed, the universe was in our corner. First-class is a world unto itself, a world that so few of us ever venture into, and a world that left me feeling like a total imposter. Not surprisingly, Rich slotted into that world beautifully. He revelled in it and he lapped it up, whereas I found the over attentive level of service slightly embarrassing. I mean, was a 12-course meal really necessary? And isn't it a bit odd for a bunch of total strangers to change into their Qantas pyjamas and slippers en masse in the middle of the day and before we have even taken off? Don't get me wrong, I wasn't complaining. That level of lavish luxury is just not entirely my style.

While I was not yet fully comfortable with my swanky high-flying surroundings, I was extremely grateful for the bed and the privacy. Two hours into our flight, Rich had to inject me in the bum with progesterone. It's an extremely thick concoction mixed with seed oil, and the pain of the progesterone shot is renowned as the worst. The needle is ridiculously thick, and it must go deep into the muscle to be effective. I'm not sure if it was the altitude or Richard's dodgy aim in that tiny aircraft toilet cubicle, but the pain that ensued was like nothing I had ever experienced from an injection. After 30 minutes, a gigantic, purple, throbbing bruise began to develop, and it was so painful that I spent the entire 14 hours unable to sleep. Instead, I watched seven movies while everyone else slumbered around me, and by the time we landed in LA, I wasn't in the best state. It had been a marathon 24 hours, and the thought of hiring a car and driving three hours to San Diego in an unfamiliar country on the wrong side of the road was way more than I could fathom. I was right on the edge of breaking down, and so my beautiful, understanding and well-rested husband, sensing my despair, suggested we hire a nearby hotel room for a few hours (hourly rate hotels were plentiful around LAX) so that I could sleep.

It was early morning in LA. Grey, busy and daunting. We caught the bus to our hire car and Rich awkwardly inched out of the car park into the crazy la-la-land peak hour traffic. I'm not sure how he managed to drive on the other side of the road in such unfamiliar surroundings with only a cinch of hesitation, but I was so grateful for his leadership. We pulled into the nearest motel, a Travelodge, and we booked a room until three in the afternoon. The motel was a dump, and a far cry from the luxury hotel in the sky we had just exited. That didn't particularly bother me after a day of no sleep, but the clientele was like nothing we had experienced before either, and it made me uneasy. I had clearly seen too many American movies, and in my clouded, vulnerable state, I found myself racially profiling a bunch of innocent African American males as potential gun-yielding criminals. My assumptions were of course ludicrous, driven by baseless fear, and I was immediately ashamed by my ignorance. Note to self: ethnic stereotyping is pathetic and unacceptable, even when one is in a shambolic, altered state. We went upstairs, and I sank into bed. I was out almost instantly, but not before checking myself. We had made it. How crazy is life? We were here in America to start a family. Neil Diamond's *We're Coming to America* played in my head for a few verses, and the next thing I knew I was awake again, feeling refreshed with five hours having passed.

[8]
Baby Utopia

I GOT UP TO jump in the shower, and the size and colour of my throbbing bum bruise made me shudder. It ached and burned, and I had no idea how I was going to inject progesterone into my backside every day if this was the aftermath. Right now, though, I needed to push through the pain and focus on getting to San Diego. We'd decided to wing it regarding where we were going to stay on this trip. Rich and I are such "vibey" people, and you can't gauge the vibe of a place via the internet. Also, being our first (and hopefully last) IVF trip, we planned to travel around a bit and do the touristy thing in the week between Richard's donation and the embryo transfer. We were so excited to be in California together, and given that everything IVF-related on this trip had to be so scheduled, structured and exact, we just wanted to see how we felt each morning, and to go with the flow when it came to our plans and our surroundings.

Once you escape the fog and the utter madness of LA traffic, the drive along the Pacific Coast Highway is fairly straight and unexpectedly scenic. Orange County is breathtakingly picturesque in places, and we passed through one little town that really captivated us. It was called Laguna Beach, and it had a unique beauty and an energy about it that we were instantly drawn to. We agreed to return there at some stage during the trip, and we rolled on to San Diego. It took us just over two hours of driving to reach the city, but then almost another two hours to find the right place to stay. We explored downtown and the Gaslamp district, but ultimately settled on a hotel in Little Italy. From there we went to dinner, I quickly retired, and Rich stayed on for another drink or two. This would set the scene for the rest of our journey. Rich has a far bigger engine than me to start with, and given I wasn't drinking at all (aside from one French champagne on the flight) I was not the party girl nor the partner in crime Rich was used to on holidays. The jury is out on whether the occasional drink while undergoing IVF has any impact on the outcome. Some doctors advise you to abstain, and after all we had been through, I wasn't about to take any chances. And so, Rich was left to enjoy our first night out in California solo, but under strict instructions from me to take it easy. He had a rather important task to undertake tomorrow.

When we arrived at the San Diego Fertility Centre the following morning, I had butterflies in my stomach. It was like a dream to finally be here, and walking in, I felt a mixture of excitement and elation. I felt like I had finally found that missing piece preventing us from realising our dreams, and here we were—we had crossed the world and finally made it to our baby utopia. Everything about SDFC felt like a big warm hug. Frankie the receptionist greeted us like we were the oldest of friends, and everyone had such a kind, sunny, relaxed California disposition. There had been so much planning involved in getting us to this point, and I felt like almost everyone I met that morning had played a part. I was so touched by the sense of warmth and the personalised attention we were receiving, and it was such a stark contrast to my experiences back home in Melbourne. We met our doctor—Dr Michael Kettel, an award-winning pioneer in the field of IVF in America—and Barbara, our delightful and caring nurse. There was nothing clinical about this place; it was cosy and inviting, and even the embryologists were relaxed and friendly.

Barbara took us into a room to update us on our donor, who was due to have her egg retrieval surgery in less than one hour. We didn't know her real name, we only knew her as DON. Like most of the girls on the register, she had chosen to be an anonymous egg donor. Barbara advised us that DON had not produced as many follicles as expected. Only ten at this stage to be exact, but they were still hopeful of a good result. I was stunned by this unexpected disclosure, especially given that even my sad, old, useless ovaries had managed to produce eight follicles. In America, they use stronger drugs than in most other countries, including Australia, so donors generally produce 20-30 follicles. This was not good news, especially if we wanted to have more than one child. The plan was to freeze as many embryos as possible after the transfer as an insurance policy in case the first transfer didn't work and to provide us with a future child from the same donor when the time came for us to have a second baby. I was instantly terrified that this news was going to mess up my perfect plan, but there was no way I would concede and allow myself to feel what

I wanted to feel deep down, which was bitter disappointment and premature defeat. I had to hang on to hope and trust that this was still going to work out just as I'd designed it in my mind.

Next, I was taken for an ultrasound and blood tests, while Rich was escorted to a private room to do his thing. I can only imagine the pressure he must have been feeling, being in that environment and knowing how high the stakes were. Despite that burden, Rich performed like a champion, and now it was up to the lovely DON. She was lovely too. I didn't know her, but I felt it. I had read and re-read her profile at least 100 times, and it was so detailed that she no longer felt like a stranger. She seemed to have a beautiful spirit and a giving nature, and more than anything she just loved being a mother. It takes a very special and altruistic person to donate their eggs. Yes, she was compensated, but $5000 in the scheme of what she had to put herself through was not a lot. IVF is so brutal! In the end they retrieved seven eggs. Barbara told me DON felt disappointed and concerned for us. I was touched by that and was now just hoping that all of the eggs would fertilise and survive to day five. Statistically this was unlikely, but there was so much more to this than science, so who knew what might happen. We were told that our embryologist would call us each day to update us on the numbers and progress of the embryos, so off we went to spend the next five days doing our best to distract ourselves from counting our chickens. And that would be no mean feat.

The next day when the call finally came, we were visiting Disneyland, my favourite place on the planet! I stood frozen in Tomorrowland holding my breath, so fearful of what she may or may not say. Five of the seven eggs had fertilised—okay. Three were graded good

good (A grade), and two were graded good fair (B grade)—okay. Hmmm. I didn't know what to feel. Neutral would be the best way to put it, or perhaps numb. I was in Disneyland, the happiest place on earth, but ironically, I felt nothing. Had this been the result of my own IVF, I would have been celebrating right now, but it wasn't, and I wasn't. Was I about to crumble in Disneyland of all places? My expectations had been extraordinarily high, and I had definitely expected more than one baby from this $60,000 journey. To have only five embryos this early on was a huge disappointment. Unfortunately, you can't predict these things, and no matter how well you plan, or how much money you invest, it's still a gamble. I had to take a moment to recalibrate and adjust my expectations. We were still in with a fighting chance, and if we are blessed with one baby and only one baby it would still be the greatest gift we had ever known.

[9]
Destino?

THE DAYS THAT FOLLOWED were such a whirlwind, a mixed bag of amazing experiences and very intense emotions. Every hour was bittersweet for me. I was living the California dream with Rich, travelling around and creating life-long memories, but also feeling so weighed down by my fear and uncertainty. It's hard to surrender to life when you've lost all control, especially when you're a control freak like me. I desperately wanted to live in the moment and relish in our experiences, but my inner child was fighting me all the way. It was like I was standing on the edge of a cliff, unsure whether I was going to fall or just savour the unforgettable adrenaline rush later. All day we would wait for the call, praying that our little embryos had survived another night and continued growing. On day three, two of our five embryos arrested. Only three remained with two days to go before transfer. It was not good news, but, of course, it could have been worse. We still had a chance, and we had to hold on to that. These embryos had to survive. If they didn't after we'd come this far, it would be nothing short of soul-destroying.

I went to bed that night and I allowed my mind to consider the alternate reality where we fly home having been denied the chance to even transfer one embryo. The fear of it was all-consuming, and I quietly cried myself to sleep, then I restlessly dreamed of my worst fears some more.

We had been all over LA and Anaheim, moving at a relentless tourist's pace. Hollywood, Disneyland, Universal Studios, Rodeo Drive, the LA Lakers—just so much to see and do. But I was so exhausted and flat by this point that we decided it was time to just settle in somewhere for the next four days. I felt so depleted physically from the IVF drugs, and utterly drained mentally from the monumental head fuck that is international IVF. I just wanted to find a cosy refuge that felt like home. So, we headed back to Laguna Beach, and what a picture-perfect, magical sanctuary that little seaside resort turned out to be. I had finally found the calming oasis my soul had been craving, and we both felt it, that very special vibe from this very special place. You can travel the world and never experience that feeling, but we felt it and we knew we had found peace. A breathtakingly beautiful, wondrous and vibrant coastal retreat filled with art galleries, scenic coves and amazing architecture.

We checked into a modest motel. It was walking distance from town and overlooking the spectacular Pacific Ocean. That view was everything. I'd never seen anything like it in real life, and until then I hadn't realised a view like that existed. It was pure, untainted heaven.

Dinner that night was at an Italian Bistro in the main street called

Alessa and our waiter was a cheerful and charismatic gentleman by the name of Rudi, who would become a familiar friend. We sat out front in the crisp Californian winter air watching the world go by, savouring the glittering street lights and the loveliness that surrounded us. We enjoyed the best seafood linguini of our lives, and I even allowed myself a half glass of red. It was almost Christmas, and as the sun went down, the annual Laguna Niguel Holiday Parade kicked off right before our eyes. The street was filled with locals, mostly families with small children running around or perched on their father's shoulders eagerly awaiting the many festive floats cruising down Forest Avenue. In that moment I thought I was living a dream, and as the tears of emotion started to flow, I thought this perfect moment in time must be a cosmic sign of more perfect moments ahead for us. It would become one of the most memorable moments of my life. A wondrous winter wonderland just swirling with hope and possibility.

The next morning it was transfer day, so we were up early and heading back down the Pacific Coast Highway to San Diego by 9.00 am. Our three remaining embryos had thankfully all survived to day five, so if all went to plan, we would have two for transfer and one for the freezer. Thank god! Before the procedure, I had acupuncture and I tried to meditate while willing and praying for our little baby's spirit to join our family. Tears streamed down my cheeks for what felt like the 100th time this trip and I was overwhelmed by the magnitude of what was about to happen. The lights were dimmed in the transfer room and it was such a warm and relaxed atmosphere. There was no full bladder required this time, and I felt more at peace than I had in a long while. Again, the polar opposite of my previous experience back home. Rich and I were in such a good place with each other, and it was great to have him there holding my hand and supporting me every step of the way. In that moment I just felt so lucky as I reflected on what we had achieved to this point. All the drugs, the steroids, the transfusions, the blood tests, the ultrasounds, the money, the travel and the dreams had led us right here to this moment in time, and it felt so right. The transfer of our two best embryos could not have gone more smoothly, and Dr Kettel said that one of the embryos transferred was a perfect ten. "That's our baby", I thought as I admired the photograph of that perfectly graded blastocyst. And we left with renewed optimism, excitement and faith that being here and living this experience had in fact been our destiny all along.

[10]
A spiritual connection

AFTER THE TRANSFER, I felt so much lighter. It was a weird but heartening feeling knowing that within just a few days I could actually be pregnant. Our nurse, Barbara, had recommended we avoid flying for a couple of days if possible, and I was more than happy to comply. We ate seafood galore, we read books and I walked or sat on the beach a lot. When I looked out across the Pacific Ocean, I felt more connected to the universe, as though doing that would somehow increase the chance of someone listening to my silent pleas. I talked to my ancestors and my guardian angels, and I prayed to them to please grant us this one colossal wish.

Rich and I have always been fairly spiritual people, and that was actually what incited our deep connection back in the mid-90s. We were both drawn to most things that promote holistic wellness or metaphysics, and we bonded over the fundamental questions in life about existence, reality and the soul. It was our belief that everything in life is pre-destined to some degree, and that our souls were likely to have had many lives prior to this one. We also believed that our children's souls had already chosen us as their parents, and it is for this reason that using an egg donor was a choice we were able to make without hesitation. It was never something we struggled with on any level, for we believe that the soul is the soul and that our child was destined to be our child, regardless of the vessel or the way in which it came to us. We knew this without question, and our parallel belief systems were one of the reasons I fell so hard and fast for Rich when we finally got together.

At this point in our lives, Rich was on a more active quest to consciously deepen his insight about life and its true purpose. And so, when he came across a little shop in Laguna called the Chakra Shack, he was immediately drawn to it. They offered psychic readings, and he felt that this would be a very fitting time to get one. Richard's business was not doing well, but he was pushing for a partnership with the world's leading business coaching firm, and if it came through it had the potential to change everything. He wanted to know about that, and about whether we would be welcoming a baby—or babies—nine months from now. Rich met with an amazing young woman by the name of Jen Raven, and he was so blown away by her energy and her accuracy that he encouraged me to book in and see her too. I did just that, and what followed would be one of the most powerful and moving experiences of my life. Jen was my age, perhaps slightly younger, and she was strikingly beautiful, but in a soft and whimsical kind of way. She had a very warm and sincere disposition, and I immediately felt that she was speaking from her heart. She must be the real deal, at least in her own mind, I thought. She was too sweet and gentle to be a charlatan. Also, she had an ethereal presence, and her intuitive and nurturing spirit was evident when she asked to hug me within the first minute of our meeting. She pulled me so close, and despite my best efforts, my tears predictably started to flow. While the crying was by no means unusual for me of late, the intensity of the emotion that washed over me in that moment was utterly overwhelming. I think I just involuntarily let go, and even the embarrassment of losing my shit in front of a stranger was not enough to control my blubbering. She just held me tighter and I was powerless to stop myself, so I just kept on crying. Not ideal given I was paying her by the minute!

Jen finally stunned me out of my state by asking if I would mind if she brought her baby in. Her baby! Not at all what I was expecting, but I agreed, now feeling slightly awkward and a little confused after so openly baring my soul. Her child was just four months old and his name was Luca, one of my favourite boys names. Luca was a gorgeous, chubby, serene little baby with a cherubic face and a delicious mop of chestnut hair. I hadn't had any real experience with babies to date, and I could count on one hand how many times I'd held one, so when Jen passed him to me and asked if I would mind holding him for the duration of our reading, I was quite overcome. Luca's skin was so soft, and he smelled heavenly. He was warm and cuddly and just so precious. As he clung to me, tears still quietly streaming down my face, it was like a switch inside of me flicked and I finally knew how it would feel to hold my own baby for the very first time, just pure love and magic. And as I listened intently to Jen's words, I felt a healing of sorts taking place that I was unaware I even needed.

I'd been so focussed on the brutal and relentless physical aspects of our journey, all the while consciously evading the real casualties in all of this, my heart and my soul. I never allowed myself to feel the pain, sorrow or loss for too long, afraid that if I did it could consume me to the point of defeat. I'd seen it happen with so many other women, and I would not allow my true feelings to prevail for long enough to deter me from marching forward. I needed to channel my inner gladiator to make this happen, and so I had allowed myself to feel the longing while resisting the deep sense of loss that I'd been slapped with so many times these past few years. The baby I lost, my extreme infertility, our failed IVFs, the doctor that failed me—I was confronted by all of that right there in Jen's little Chakra Shack, and it was cathartic to set my authentic self free for a while.

To be honest I can't recall much of what Jen said to me that day; however, I do remember her saying I would get pregnant this time, and that she felt there was a little soul around me that was eager to be born. That gave me great reassurance and I believed her wholeheartedly. After our encounter I thought for sure she was genuine because I had felt something so profound. Her energy was awe-inspiring and like nothing I had ever come across despite visiting numerous psychic mediums and spiritual healers in the past. And as for little Luca, well, he just opened my heart and made me want to meet our baby even more.

[11]
Cheers to Laguna

WE STAYED A FEW more days in our lovely little Laguna bubble, and by the time we boarded the plane from LAX home to Melbourne, I was feeling very confident. Unfortunately, I still had another week to wait for my blood test, but that is, of course, if I chose to wait. Doctors always recommend that you wait until the blood test, but thanks to Dr Google and thousands of women across the world, I now knew that it was possible to see a faint positive line on a first response home pregnancy test as early as three days after transferring a five-day-old embryo. There was no way I was going to wait another week and then spend an entire day waiting for a nurse to call me with MY news. This was not my first rodeo, and by testing myself at a time and in the surroundings of my choice, I somehow felt more empowered. I never wanted to relive an experience like the one I had when Louise called me to advise that our IVF had failed. This time I would control the circumstances, and it would just be Rich and I. I was already three days post transfer, but I decided to wait a few more days to give myself a better chance of testing positive.

Once we got home, we jumped straight back into life. Work was busier than ever, and I had several big projects on the go in the lead-up to Christmas. December is always the best time of year for us, so there was no holiday hangover, and as amazing as our experience was, I was glad to be home in our cosy shack with our beloved Boxer Bella living the everyday life that we loved. We arrived home on the Monday and I ended up waiting until Friday night to take the home pregnancy test. That way if the result was negative, I had the weekend to recover before being back in the office. I peed on the stick and gave it to Rich to read while I squeezed my eyes shut and held my breath in anticipation. I was prepared to wait a few minutes before a result, but Rich immediately declared that he could see two lines. Two lines! Two lines! I'd seen enough one-lined, negative test results to last a lifetime, so hearing those words was kind of shocking, but also not totally unexpected. Deep down I think I already knew I was pregnant, but now it was official. Our perseverance had prevailed and our crazy jaunt across the world had succeeded so spectacularly that it almost felt too good to be true. It worked, first time. First time! Thank you, thank you, angels.

Over the next few days, I told everyone close to me our incredible news. I was so confident that nothing could go wrong, and I felt like the cat that got the cream again. This time I knew our outcome would be different because they weren't my crappy old eggs. We'd used the indestructible eggs of a 24-year-old mother, and we had literally crossed the world to get them. Also, I had symptoms and I already felt SO pregnant, so what could possibly go wrong? The day of my blood test, I was as cool as a cucumber. I took the test on my way to work and I emailed Dr Nick's office manager, Tracey, to let her know that I would call her at 4.45pm when I got home for the result. I already knew I was pregnant, so my biggest concern that day was how high the HCG result would be. If it's really high, it can be an indication of twins. My mind was exploding at the thought of having two babies at once, and I wasn't sure how we would handle that. Still, I thought, there were benefits to twins, the most notable being that our family would be complete in one go and I would never have to go through that hideous IVF process again. So much to consider!

When I called Tracey, she sounded a bit rattled, but I didn't immediately catch on to her vibe. She said my HCG was only 40, but that it could be a matter of the dates being off. She asked whether I was I sure it was a day-five embryo that was transferred? And was I completely sure it had been nine days since the transfer? Her words danced around dates and numbers, but they were completely drowned out by my own thoughts. There was no grey area to cling to here. There had been no mistakes with the times or the dates, and there was no question that an HCG of 40 was a big, fat, motherfucking failure.

"How could this happen?" I thought. The combo of Richard's super sperm with DON's pristine eggs and my perfectly prepped body was supposed to equal an almost guaranteed golden ticket to success. I was totally floored by this news, and it just didn't make any sense. We had done everything right, and with militant precision. I'd even gone on a fertility diet in the months leading up to our trip. I'd taken every supplement, consumed mountains of Chinese herbs, had pins stuck in my body on a weekly basis, grown hair in strange places from high doses of steroids and been pumped so full of hormones that they took me to the brink of emotional combustion. In life, some things just aren't meant to fail, and in my mind, international egg donor IVF to the value of $60,000 fell into that category.

Tracey told me Dr Nick would call me later that evening when he had finished with patients, and as I hung up the phone, all I could see was our glittering Christmas tree and the disappointment we would be delivering to everyone that had supported us this year. I cried for them briefly, but I was surprised by my own resilience. I mean, in all honesty, what can you do? I felt angry at the world, but at the end of the day I had two choices. Lose my shit completely or accept what I can't change and move forward. I wasn't sure how I would feel when it all sank in, but for now I just wanted to open a bottle of wine with Rich and listen to Rod Stewart in our beautiful garden with our fur baby Bella. Being able to drink really was the only upside, and so, we did just that, and we toasted to our impending return to our beloved Laguna Beach. A life without despair is a life without hope, right? And so it was.

[12]
Is this Rock Bottom?

DR NICK EXPLAINED TO me that even the most flawless looking embryos created from young, fertile donors will fail fifty percent of the time, but that we can increase those odds by transferring two embryos (which we did) and by genetically testing the embryos, which was something to consider for the future if the opportunity arose.

I spoke with Barbara and requested an urgent conference call with Dr Kettel. It was December 22nd and I couldn't bear the thought of waiting until January for a conversation that would undoubtedly determine our next steps. I needed to get the baby ball rolling again, pronto. It was our assumption that I would return to San Diego in mid-January for the transfer of our one and only remaining frozen embryo; however, when Dr Kettel called the following morning, he surprised me by advising that this would likely be a waste of time since they had already transferred the two best embryos without success. He said that while one embryo had initially implanted, it had died early on, most likely due to a chromosomal abnormality, and he felt it would be smarter to start fresh with a new donor. Specifically, someone that had donated before, resulting in a number of successful pregnancies for their egg donor recipients. This is where our guarantee program turned out to be a godsend. They would refund the $40,000 in full and cover most of the costs for the new donor's IVF cycle. Once refunded, we had to return the money for a new cycle with a new donor, but our major out of pocket expenses were now just the donor's fee, my drugs and our travel expenses. Still a huge investment, but achievable if we again relied on our credit cards.

The next step was to select our donor, and we made that decision with ease. I was no longer concerned about choosing someone tall, attractive and with similar features to me. I just needed to find someone proven, and one girl in particular really stood out for that reason. Her donor name was BYR, and she had donated her eggs three times, with all three cycles resulting in successful pregnancies, two of those three resulting in twins.

She ticked every box regarding her family's health history, and she came across as a kind, intelligent, driven individual with similar values to us. The only downside was that she wasn't available until March, which felt like a lifetime at this point, but we had waited this long, so really what was two more months? Her fee was double that of the first donor (10K) due to her outstanding history of success, but again, it seemed like a small price to pay in the scheme of things, so we locked her in—and we continued to cite what had become an almost daily mantra - you just can't put a price on family.

I wish I could say that I remained stoic and upbeat over the Christmas break, but sadly it was quite the opposite. We went to my sister-in-law Shannon's house in Geelong for Christmas Eve, and that afternoon I got my period. It was not exactly the Christmas gift I'd hoped for, and the pain was intolerable. So much so that I skipped Christmas Eve dinner all together, instead opting to curl up in a ball on Shannon's bed feeling wretched, miserable and shaky since I was also suffering withdrawals from the steroids. That night, Shannon had a full house, so we had to sleep on a blow-up mattress in the lounge room. Zero privacy. My period was so heavy that I had to use the bathroom numerous times throughout the night, and in the morning, my father-in-law complained that he'd had no sleep since someone rude and insensitive had insisted on continually flushing the toilet! I was mortified, and I wanted to disappear. If only he had known, he would have been the first to put his arms around me, but it was all just too awkward and uncomfortable for me to share.

Christmas Day lunch was spent at my dad and Amanda's house. I felt marginally better being in more familiar territory, but I still opted to leave very early, while Rich stayed on to continue his annual tradition of consuming very expensive bottles of quality wine with my dad and my uncle John.

I couldn't deny the fact that I felt gutted by our set back, and I felt so raw and emotionally drained that I found it hard to pretend otherwise. My walls had come down since meeting with Jen, and I didn't have the strength nor the motivation to build them back up again. I wanted to feel the pain and process everything in private, rather than having to put on my cheerful Christmas front. Today of all days was not the day to burden anyone with my troubles, and no one else deserved to be dragged down with me. All I wanted right now was to be home in my bed with chocolate, red wine and my devoted dog, Bella. I just needed a few days to grieve in peace, then I could dust myself off and charge forward like I always did.

I returned to work after the break and for the most part life went back to normal. I continued with the acupuncture, the fertility diet and the supplements, and when I wasn't at work, I'd busy myself with the planning of our impending return to America. Dr Kettel requested that I have my endometrial lining tested for the presence of the beta-3 integrin protein, a strong indicator of uterine receptivity. Basically, if the protein is present, your uterus is probably good to go, and if it's not, then your uterus will struggle to accept a transferred embryo. The test could only be conducted at a laboratory in California at the time, and so Dr Nick had to read up on the procedure to familiarise himself on what was required of him. From there I would have to FedEx my tissue across the world in a liquid filled canister for preservation. Getting the sample was supposed to be the easy part, but I had absolutely no idea what I was walking into, and little did I know, I was about to experience the worst pain of my life.

I hadn't bothered to read up on the procedure itself. I'd had many invasive procedures to date and this one seemed straight forward enough—I assumed it was just like a pap smear. I was so very wrong! The pain as Dr Nick suctioned out the tissue sample from my uterus was beyond excruciating, so much so that I almost passed out. And while in the past I had always appreciated Nick's unwaveringly direct, no-nonsense approach, in that moment I could have done with just a little more empathy! I left his office speechless and pale as a ghost, and I think I was in complete shock for a few hours afterwards. When I got home I even vomited twice, and this is coming from a girl with a very high pain threshold. It was only then that I bothered to google other people's experiences, and as I read on in horror, I realised that it was probably best that I went in completely blind not knowing what I was in for. You know the pain must be next level when it literally makes you sick. Where was the anaesthetic? Or at the very least, a pre-scrape Valium to absorb some of the shock!

Once I pulled it together, I had to take the little canister with my sample inside off to the local Fed Ex office to be shipped to California. I had never sent a Fed Ex before, and I was surprised by the amount of paperwork and formalities required. Once I handed my completed forms over and they read that I was sending human tissue overseas, shit hit the fan a little bit, and I had to wait over an hour while the staff made phone calls and trawled through handbooks. They were speaking hastily in another language, and while I could see they were perplexed by my request, they were determined to make it happen for me, which I truly appreciated. They probably thought I had a rare disease. Apparently, no one had attempted to send a sample of their own body tissue overseas from this shop before. It was unprecedented! In a strange kind of way that made me feel proud like I was a bit of a trailblazer. Pushing the boundaries beyond the status quo and leaving no stone unturned in my efforts to procreate. Eventually I got the green light to send the package, and after a few anxious days of waiting, the results came through and all was in check with me. I felt relieved and reassured, and it was the little lift I needed to forge ahead with renewed confidence. Now nothing was standing in our way.

[13]
An Altruistic Angel

March 2013

Our departure day arrived quickly, and I felt calmer, more prepared and further equipped emotionally this time around. Getting a seat on the plane wasn't down to the wire, and we were issued with confirmed business-class seats at check-in. No panic attacks to speak of! The drug side effects were not quite so ghastly, and Rich had now mastered the progesterone injection so the flight over was more comfortable. Once we arrived in LA, I didn't feel as much like a sleep-deprived maniac as last time, so were able to head straight to San Diego in preparation for Richard's sperm donation the following day. Our new donor had already had an ultrasound to check her follicles, and at last count she had over 40, so we were on track for an exceptional result. I felt the tides turning, and in my mind, there was no doubt that this time it was going to work.

I was ecstatic to be back here in such beautiful Californian coastal surroundings again, and this time we opted to keep things simple and stay close to the clinic until the transfer. We chose a boutique hotel in La Jola Village as our home for the next few days, and again we were so impressed by all that this little seaside town had to offer. I slept peacefully that night knowing that we were so close I could smell it, and the following morning when we arrived at SDFC, I felt ready to take on the world.

When we walked in, I was surprised by how full the waiting room was. There were probably at least ten couples in there, and a few of the guys were standing due to a lack of seating. As we got settled I was encouraged by the fact that there appeared to be other international travellers waiting alongside us. Most of the couples were either speaking with heavy accents or in another language, and I immediately felt a strong sense of comradery with all of them. We were far from alone in this contest against nature, and being here with others like us was a stark reminder that this journey of ours was by no means unique.

When Frankie called us up she explained that this was an unusually busy morning and that there was currently quite a long wait for the two private "donation" rooms. The only alternative was the powder room, which Rich reluctantly agreed to. Frankie handed Rich his specimen jar and directed him to the powder room, which unfortunately you can only enter via the nurses' station. I was quite embarrassed for my husband, but he sucked it up and got the job done nonetheless. Such a trooper! In the meantime, I went in for my ultrasound, and I was a little taken aback when Barbara told me that my endometrium lining was nine centimetres thick. That was two centimetres less than last time. Not a deal breaker by any means, but in IVF it's generally a matter of the thicker the better. A thicker lining is considered more receptive and nourishing, and for an IVF embryo transfer to be successful, it's crucial that your lining be a minimum of seven to eight millimetres. I was confused as to why it would be different this time when I'd done everything the same. I felt slightly nervous and uncertain initially, but I was assured that this wasn't an issue and I chose to shake it off and trust the experts. After all, I felt in my heart that this time it would work.

Before I left, I handed Barbara a letter I had written for our donor, which she promised to deliver to her immediately since she was already on site being prepped for her egg retrieval. This was what it said:

To the lovely BYR,

It's taken me a while to write this letter, purely because it's difficult for us to articulate our level of gratitude in words.

From day one we were thrilled to learn that you had accepted as our donor, particularly after the heartbreak of learning that our first cycle had failed. We feel that there are a lot of nuances between us, and you come across as an amazing, intelligent, positive and active person who lives life to the fullest.

Your kind and selfless gesture is beyond life-changing for not only Rich and me, but also for our entire family, who have all been on this journey with us. We all feel that you are now also part of our family in some way, and I've spent many hours wondering about you and your life. So, I thought I'd share a little bit about us with you. That way if you ever wonder, you will know more about who your incredible gift has benefited.

My name is Kristen. I'm 36 and I'm married to my best friend and soulmate Richard. We met at kindergarten and came back into each other's lives at the age of 15 when we met again on the school bus. From there we became and remained extremely close friends. Rich played professional football (Australian Rules) for many years, and so he spent 12 years travelling and playing all over Australia. We stayed in very close contact during these years, but it wasn't until we were reunited at a wedding in Bali in 2008 that we fell in love.

I work for Qantas as an account manager (which is very helpful when you are travelling back and forth from San Diego) and Rich now has his own business as a leadership coach for elite sports people (we were thrilled to read that your dad is a coach)! We live in a beautiful bayside suburb in Melbourne. We have an amazing family, and the greatest group of friends you could ever wish for. Both of our parents were divorced when we were very young, so we now have seven parents between us! Thankfully everyone gets along famously, and we often have family events all together. We are also BIG animal lovers. We have a one-year-old Boxer Lab cross called Bella who we miss terribly. She is the light of my life!

After 18 months of marriage, and several failed IVFs, we learned that having children that were genetically linked to me would likely be impossible. Unfortunately, adoption in Australia is also not an option. Many Australians wait eight years or more without success. For us, egg donation was a perfect solution, and San Diego appealed to us because of the high rate of success and the fact that we could learn things about our chosen donor. My brother is adopted, so the loss of genetics was irrelevant to us. We know that for our family, biology is inconsequential. Once the decision was made, we never looked back.

There was something about you BYR that resonated with us, and so the donor decision was easy. You and I share many of the same qualities. We have no doubt that this is all meant to be, and we feel extremely lucky to have been given this amazing opportunity to have our own family. Having been through IVF, I know how difficult it is, so thank you. Thank you from the bottom of our hearts for putting yourself through this gruelling process, not just once, but numerous times. It must be an amazing feeling to know how you have made such a life-changing impact on so many people.

I want you to know that we intend to let our child/children know the story of how they came to us, and you are such a big and integral part of that story. They will know everything that we know about you.

This is a big week for you. We will be thinking of you and

we hope you recover well.

All our love and eternal gratitude.

Kristen and Richard xxxxxx

[14]
The Prince of the Party

WE HEADED BACK TO La Jolla that afternoon, and we were over the moon when we got the call that they had retrieved 27 mature eggs from our donor. It was an unbelievable result, and it felt like we had hit the jackpot. We were so freaking fortunate! Initially it was hard to grasp how significant this result was for us, but once it had fully sunk in, I was able to accept that it was unlikely we would ever need to engage an egg donor again, and that felt truly amazing. Such a different experience to last time. All my fears just melted away.

We now had six days of waiting to see how many embryos developed to day five. I wasn't so concerned this time, as I knew we would likely end up with more embryos than we would ever use, but it would still be a tense time and it was all about getting the quality along with the quantity. I wasn't really feeling it in La Jolla, so we decided on a change of scene and we headed to Pacific Beach. It had a more relaxed, surfy vibe than La Jolla, and more importantly, it was cheaper. It was also full of teenagers due to it being Spring Break at the time. Not quite what I was expecting from this restful escape, but I didn't think they would bother us, and the crowds added to the atmosphere. The more the merrier was always my motto in life! We checked into a simple, oceanfront motel room for the week and we settled into our temporary abode. This time we wouldn't be moving around, sight-seeing or doing the touristy thing. We were both here to work, and this was not a holiday. I was lucky to have an understanding boss and a flexible job that I could perform remotely, and Rich was in the same flexi-boat running his own business. We started work very early each morning as the spring breakers were just coming home from their wild nights out, and we would finish around lunch time, allowing us the afternoons to chill, walk on the beach and explore the neighbourhood. It was all about early nights, delicious seafood and clean living for me, and the time just flew by.

The day after the egg retrieval, our embryologist called us with the incredible news that nineteen eggs had successfully fertilised and were going strong. We were ecstatic! By day three, we still had nineteen embryos looking great, which was almost unheard of, and on transfer day we were astonished to learn that seventeen were still on track to either transfer or freeze. That had to be a freaking record!

The morning of the transfer I was relaxed and very excited. I couldn't wait to get to back SDFC, which had come to feel like a beloved second home to me. I adored the feeling of being cared for by so many kind and charismatic people that clearly appreciated the fact that we had travelled halfway across the world to work with them. I felt like they were all genuinely rooting for us, and the level of attention, warmth and sincerity they offered me was just so enriching and comforting. That may sound weird, but I left home at the age of nineteen, and being a grown-up can be exhausting and overwhelming at times. It's nice to feel nurtured, especially by so many people at once. I know we were paying them a small fortune for that privilege, but at the time I was also convinced that they all had a huge soft spot for me and considered me an extra special case.

Dr Kettel wasn't working that day as our transfer date had fallen on a weekend this time around. I was disappointed by this, but our stand-in doctor was lovely and more than qualified. She was happy with the appearance of the two embryos selected, and the transfer went beautifully. My lining had even grown another millimetre which was very encouraging. Afterwards we drove straight to Laguna Beach to spend the next couple of days in our special little paradise while we waited for the embryos to hopefully attach. Implantation normally occurs 48-72 hours after transfer, so I was adamant that I couldn't fly home until at least three days had passed. Even though the studies were inconclusive, I was certain that the altitude would not be doing our embryos any favours, and I needed to know that attachment would have already occurred before I boarded my plane.

I didn't feel great during the drive from San Diego to Laguna, and suddenly, my mental state shifted. We stopped for lunch at a rooftop restaurant with the most breathtaking views, but I felt anxious and out of sorts and I couldn't shift my mood, so we left to find a place to stay. I just needed to rest my head. This time we chose Hotel Laguna, an iconic art deco hotel built in the 1930s. It was situated in the heart of town, and it had the most amazing views.

Unfortunately, the room they gave us wasn't cutting it for me. It was an old, cold shoe box, with white walls, red carpet and an eerie energy. In my normal state, I would have insisted we move on, but I was overcome by all that had led us to this point, and right now I felt like there was nothing left in me. I needed to stop. And so, there we stayed.

After a quick power nap I felt a bit brighter, so we went downstairs to the hotel's beach club and Rich surprised me by ordering a Long Island Iced Tea. He didn't drink spirits at that time, and in all our years of knowing each other, I'd never seen him order a cocktail, let alone a cocktail that contained five different spirits! In hindsight, Rich was probably just trying to deal with the enormous pressure he was under, but he was far too cool and noble to let on with me in such a fragile state, and at the time I was so wrapped up in my own world that I just assumed he wanted to celebrate. How nice for him! I thought in my begrudgingly sarcastic sober state. I wasn't at all in the mood to watch my husband get plastered, but that's exactly what happened, and when he befriended the couple on the next table and invited them to join us, my blood really started to boil. I wasn't interested in making new friends today, and I definitely wasn't in the mood to befriend a couple of drinking buddies!

What ensued was several hours of increasingly weird conversation, followed by a clearly inebriated Rich accepting an unexpected invitation from our new-found friends to head to another bar nearby. I respectfully declined the offer, preferring to retire to our creepy room for a night of cable TV, lobster rolls (soooo good) and French fries. In the meantime, Rich, who had been coerced into taking a cab ride about 20 kilometres inland to a very dodgy bar and had sobered up along the way, had come to the realisation that his new-found friends, and the friends of said friends, were all super strange, and that he probably needed to bolt. He tells me through scattered memory that he ended up at a dilapidated night club with black walls where everyone, aside from the barman, suddenly disappeared. He promptly exited and found his wobbly way home to me.

[15]
Hotel Riviera

THE FOLLOWING MORNING WHILE I was having breakfast, Rich (feeling dusty but ever the champion nonetheless) went for a run up the hill to check out some other hotels in the area. I'd made it abundantly clear that I wanted out of this place pronto, and after last night's strange antics, Rich felt the same way. He found us a kitsch and casual beachfront hotel called The Laguna Riviera Resort, and he returned to me so chuffed and enthused by his discovery. Built in the late 1940s, its classic original features oozed character, and most of the rooms had stunning panoramic views across the Pacific and out to Catalina Island. I was so relieved to leave the creepy hotel with the bad juju, and this place had a completely contrary feel to it. So warm, charming and friendly with its tropical gardens, and almost every external wall adorned in colourful murals by local artists. This place was perfect, and it made my heart sing. That might sound over the top to some, but I'm all about getting my surroundings right, and I felt an instant connection to this funny old mid-century modern building. My only regret was that we were heading back to LA the following day and that we hadn't found this place sooner.

Our room was small and simple, but the views were spectacular, and the sound of the ocean crashing against the rocks below us was deeply cathartic. It was nice to bask in that serenity and regain some mental momentum after a rocky day yesterday, and I suddenly felt compelled to contact Jen for another reading. I hadn't spoken to her since our last visit, but we had communicated several times via email, and I now felt quite connected to her. She booked me in for later that afternoon at the Chakra Shack, and as I walked to our meeting, I dared to question whether she would level with me if the news was bad.

When I saw Jen again, I instantly sensed her nurturing energy enfold me and she embraced me with such familiarity, warmth and love. Clearly, she was a special human, and I was so glad I'd reached out to her. The session ended up being more about healing than predicting the future, though clearly that was what I was there for. She talked a lot about energy, and she said she felt the presence of two baby souls around me, hoping to be born in the very near future. In our last few moments I was still impatiently needing answers, so I just came out and asked her whether I would achieve a successful pregnancy from this trip. I clearly recall her stumbling over her answer. She subtly danced around the question, and there was no emphatic or solid response, no direct yes, and no sense of relief from my perspective. And then she said, "If it weren't to work this trip, it will definitely work next trip, so whatever you do, don't give up on those babies—they're so close". And there it was again, that funny, slightly off feeling I hadn't been able to shake since the trip back here. My heart sank, and I left feeling disturbingly empty.

On my walk home to Riviera, I replayed all of Jen's words in my head, desperately trying to decipher what she had really meant. It all felt so muddy and confusing, and not at all what I had expected. I wanted clarity, confirmation and complete reassurance. I had received none of that, and to me, Jen's mortal responses suggested that she just didn't have the answers this time. Maybe she wasn't the real deal after all, maybe the universe doesn't reveal itself always in all ways, or maybe she was just a beautiful soul that didn't want to burst my bubble and share the cold hard truth, that it just wasn't going to work this time.

That night we had a fairly sombre final dinner in our beloved Laguna. I tried to remain upbeat, but I was filled with anxiety about what had transpired with Jen, and about the fact that Rich would be leaving me in LA tomorrow night to travel home to Melbourne one day before me. Not only were we leaving our happy place, but we were separating. I was so conflicted about whether to stay behind, but I knew I would kick myself if I flew before my magic 72 hours post-transfer time restriction and the IVF then failed, and Rich had to get home for an important meeting that simply couldn't be rescheduled. He was my security and he had been by my side throughout every step of this international IVF process. I was afraid to be alone with myself and with my thoughts, and though I had travelled alone all over the world for work over the years, the thought of coming home solo from this trip just terrified me.

The next morning, we drove back to LA with the plan of finding accommodation close to the airport. I had spent many months living and working in LA on and off over the years, and I wanted to head somewhere that felt safe and familiar. For me that place was Hermosa Beach, another beachfront city in the South Bay region of LA County. I had always stayed there on my work trips, and it was only 15 minutes from LAX. Before we got settled, we had lunch on the pier and Rich happily made conversation with the locals. I think he was oblivious to the level of angst I was feeling. How could he know? I'd always been a fiercely independent free spirit. In this moment, though, I barely recognised that girl I once was. I felt like I was about to implode.

After lunch we headed to the hotel and Rich made sure I was settled before heading to the airport. I cried when he left, and it was probably the most alone I'd felt in years. I stayed hauled up in that room for the next 24 hours, only getting out of bed to order room service. I listened to my body intently, searching for that now familiar feeling that I knew was possibly the start of something. I'd only been pregnant twice, but both times I felt like I knew before I took the pregnancy test. It's a feeling you get that you'll always second guess, but it's there, and after my last five-day embryo transfer I felt those tell tail symptoms before the plane had even landed back in Melbourne. Faint cramps in the abdomen, breasts starting to hurt near the armpits, and just generally feeling a little bit off. This time though, as much as I examined and scrutinised every twinge, the reality was, I felt nothing. The nothingness engulfed me, and it just felt so ominous. I was so drained and exhausted from all my mental what-the-fuckery, and I wondered how I could already feel so deflated without knowing the outcome. Looking back, deep down, I think my intuition had already conceded. I had almost given up on this cycle, and potentially also on the whole fucking thing. Nothing in life should be this hard and feel this bad, especially not the creation of life itself.

[16] When the Stars Align

ONCE SAFELY BACK IN Melbourne, I took a pregnancy test almost immediately—against Richard's very firm counsel, mind you. It was early, most likely too early, but I did it anyway, and I took one every night after that right up until my blood test. Every day the negative result just reaffirmed what I already knew in my heart, and on the day of the blood test, I can't say I even felt disappointed when my nurse called with the result. There was no glimmer of hope. She was just ticking a box I had already ticked, and I had already grieved. Now I just wanted to move on to the next step, whatever that may be.

I threw myself back into life with passion and conviction. A seed of doubt had been planted, and I wanted to embrace all things non-baby for the first time in a while. Work, friends, family and Rich all became my priorities, and subconsciously I think I needed the validation of knowing that we could lead a rich and fulfilling life without children. All the while we were surrounded by friends having babies, but I can't say I ever felt jealous or resentful. I was so happy for my friends; they all deserved to be parents just as much as we did, and at the end of the day, we didn't want their baby. We wanted our own.

A few weeks passed before I could meet with Dr Kettel over the phone as he was actually in Australia at an international IVF conference. This was very frustrating, but I was able to see Dr Nick in the meantime for his synopsis of what may have gone wrong.

Dr Nick acknowledged that there was now a probable cause for concern, and when we finally spoke, Dr Kettel concurred. Dr Nick wanted me to up the ante with my autoimmune and natural killer cell treatments, and so he suggested I try IVIG on top of the Intralipid transfusions I was already doing.

IVIG (Intravenous Immunoglobulin) is a controversial treatment that administers a mixture of human antibodies and human blood plasma intravenously to suppress the killer cells that can damage the root system of the embryo, resulting in immediate rejection or early pregnancy loss. Both Intralipid and IVIF therapies have been shown to normalise the killing power of natural killer cells in the blood; however, most doctors believed that the cheaper and more convenient Intralipid therapy (which is derived from soy) offers a sufficient level of treatment. A dose of Intralipids costs around $40, whereas a dose of IVIG cost closer to $2,500, but who was I to argue with Dr Nick? I believed (then and now) that the man was a genius, and I loved that he would go to greater lengths than most to ensure success. It was a small price to pay in the scheme of what we were doing, but still a huge investment that was difficult to swallow. I was going to need to pay Dad and Amanda another visit, and I hoped that a loan wasn't out of the question.

Dr Nick felt strongly about the fact that "the issue was rarely the oven", whereas Dr Kettel felt that my uterus still required additional focus. I took both doctors' advice on board, and in the end, I was locked in for another FedEx'd endometrial lining test, Intralipids pre and post transfer, IVIG pre and post transfer, a much higher dose of steroids to suppress my immune system further, acupuncture, supplements, Chinese herbs and enough IVF drugs to make your eyes water.

Things were good at home; we had resumed our happy little life and work was pumping. So, when I received an unexpected call direct from Dr Kettel saying that we needed to get on a plane urgently while my endometrial lining showed the presence of the much-needed Beta 3 Integrin protein (as its presence can apparently vary from month to month) I felt completely unprepared.

I had already been put on the pill in preparation for this day, and if I started the drugs immediately the transfer could occur in just two weeks, but it was all just theoretical up until now, and I couldn't have imagined that things would move this fast. My head was reeling, and by far my biggest challenge was breaking the news to my boss. While he had been nothing short of amazing up to this point, there certainly had to be a point where I pushed the envelope too far, and I was pretty sure I was now at that point. I worked in an all-male sales team (excluding myself) which I didn't think worked in my favour in terms of their level of understanding, and I had already used up all of my holidays jetting back and forth to

America these past six months. So, when he gave me the green light and said I could again work remotely from the US, I was floored. My boss confided in me, sharing that he and his wife had also struggled with infertility before having their two daughters, and I was truly humbled by his empathy and compassion. The stars, it seemed, had aligned yet again, and maybe, just maybe, this time our luck would take us all the way.

Less than two weeks later and we would be back in our beloved Laguna at the Riviera Resort. And, as fast as that fire in my belly had extinguished, it was reignited again. This time with renewed optimism, determination and vigour, and shining more brightly than ever before. The human spirit is hard to kill, and mine was more defiant and more governing than I ever could have imagined. I suppose we don't know our own will until it is truly tested, and mine had never been tested to the nth degree like this. It was only now that I realised what I was capable of, and it was invigorating to reach the realisation that I can control my own mindset and push through my fears to get to the other side of my true self. I wasn't trudging back into battle either, I was totally skipping! I was back, baby, and this time I really meant business.

[17] The Glue That Holds Us Together

May 2013

Dr Kettel wasn't mucking around either, and on the day of the transfer he told me they were going to try something extra called embryo glue, which is a simple, low-cost additive that I now know has a proven implantation-enhancing effect, significantly increasing the chance of a live birth. At the time, I was perplexed, and I wished my two doctors had pulled out all the stops on day one, but I figured they mustn't usually need the whole bag of tricks, and that all these little extras were only reserved for the very tricky cases like mine. Now that I know what I know, I can't believe it's not standard practice for every IVF transfer, especially when the patient is travelling halfway across the world!

It felt like everything was falling into place again on this trip but in a deeper and clearer way this time. I felt it with more conviction, and I couldn't believe how much more I had learned about my body and the overall process since our last visit. The IVIG in particular made so much sense to me. I had autoimmune issues that caused my body to attack an embryo before it had a chance to thrive. By filling my body with platelets from thousands of other human beings, I imagined my immune system would feel confused, distracted and preoccupied. Hopefully just too busy with everyone else invading my body to notice a tiny embryo or two just doing their thing. I felt enlightened, with a resonant path, and you know what they say about knowledge and power.

The transfer was flawless, enjoyable even. Dr Kettel seemed to take extra care to talk us through every moment, and we laughed and joked throughout the process as though we were old friends catching up over dinner. The nurses and embryologists were all as beautiful and kind as always, but today it felt like they were going even further out of their way to demonstrate their genuine optimism and hope for a successful pregnancy this time around. Everyone was clearly rooting for us, and I felt so supported in that cosy cocoon. It's still hard for me to believe that a medical facility of that calibre exists, with the most authentically caring and compassionate team of professional humans I've ever encountered.

Rich and I felt like total California pros now too, and we had the journey and the destinations down to a low-stress fine art. We had evolved beyond the hire car from LAX and the aimless searching for accommodation in the right place with the right vibe. This time we had a car collect us and deliver us directly to Laguna Beach, where our specifically requested room at the Riviera Resort was pre-booked for an early check-in. Everything felt seamless, and my thoughts rarely drifted to the dark side. We were in the best place as a couple and our relationship was thriving. IVF can tear relationships apart, but this experience had only strengthened ours thus far. I felt lucky, strong, confident and ready. This absolutely had to be our time.

The night of the transfer it felt like we were celebrating; like we were already counting our chickens, which was a curious jump given last time everything had started to feel so dark and questionable for me at this point. Was the human mind just a fickle little trickster? I couldn't and still can't pinpoint why things felt so radically different that night, but I'll never forget how much our spirits were flying. Dr Kettel had insisted that I take a walk and have a glass of red wine when we got back to Laguna, and I jumped at the opportunity. I had been ordered to relax and have fun, and who was I to argue with my doctor! We strolled along the cliffs beholding the most mystical sunset, before finding our perfect al fresco position at an outdoor Mexican clifftop restaurant and bar called Las Brisas. I remember feeling so blessed and fulfilled as I took in that magical view and savoured every sip of my Pinot Noir. And as Rich and I marvelled over our life and just how extraordinarily far we had come, we said a little prayer, asking our baby-to-be's soul to please join our family, and asking the universe and our ancestors to help guide our little baby's soul home.

In the days that followed we explored every corner of Laguna, and we savoured every moment of our time there, trusting that this would be our last visit here—at least for a few years. It was bittersweet. I grappled with whether to see Jen this time, but in the end my curiosity prevailed, and I cautiously paid her a visit. I need not have worried, though; Jen was distinctively different this time around. She spoke with great certainty about the future, and the only thing she was unclear on was whether we were going to have one baby or two! It was a joyously validating catch up, and again I felt nostalgic as we embraced and said our farewells. I cherished the time we had spent together, and I held Jen dear to my heart, just as I now held Laguna, our journey and all the people that had touched our lives along the way dear to my heart. This whole experience now felt pre-destined, necessary and like something we would likely look back on with gratitude and fondness.

By the time we got back on that plane home to Melbourne, I just knew that this transfer had taken. My boobs hurt like crazy and my tummy was crampy. I couldn't wait to get back and take a pregnancy test. It was Thursday now, only five days post transfer. I waited till Sunday to test, and as soon as I did, two faint lines instantly appeared. Oh my god, YESSSSSSSSSSSSSSSSSSSS!

[18]
No Maybe This Time, Baby

IN THE LEAD-UP TO my blood test, I wasn't taking any chances. I needed to know that my HCG hormone levels were where they should be, so I purchased a bunch of Clear Blue digital pregnancy tests that told me how far along I was, and I used one every morning to ensure my HCG level wasn't reducing. I was obsessed, and that little morning ritual allowed me to go about my day with some level of comfort and protection from my runaway mind. That Friday was my 37th birthday, and it was one of my happiest. We went to a local pub with a small group of our best friends, and I recall the way I felt that night as though it were yesterday. I was euphoric, blissed out and just so totally fulfilled. I didn't care that I couldn't drink—I was so high on life, and I loved who I was for the first time in a while. In my mind I was the luckiest girl alive that day, and I loved how it felt to be pregnant at last. It was as though

I'd finally been invited to join an exclusive club for accomplished women that had repeatedly rejected my membership requests till now. And as shallow as it may sound, I felt like I was special, and maybe even a little superior to everyone else there that night.

The day before the blood test, my Clearblue went from reading two-three weeks to four-five weeks— validation at last! It was one of the happiest days of my life. I was pregnant, and this little embryo was moving in the right direction. It felt so amazing to know that there was a little life inside of me, and right now I was certain that this one (or two) would go the distance. I took the blood test on the way to work and I didn't even fall to pieces when my nurse failed to get back to me until the following day. Thanks to those digital tests that I was continuing to use daily, I knew that I would likely be okay. And I was okay. More than okay. My HCG levels came back at 144. A very acceptable number indeed. I had a script to take the HCG test again in two days and I'd been told they needed the number to double in that period to indicate that the pregnancy is viable. It did, and we were excited beyond words. I could finally find some peace in the knowledge that THIS WAS ACTUALLY HAPPENING!

Once the dust settled, I wish I could tell you that my inner peace triumphed, and I wholly embraced my pregnancy. Throughout our years of infertility, my idealist mind had constructed a perfect fantasy where I'd be skipping through the days looking stunning and emulating love and light throughout my pregnancy, but that was far from the case, and my short-lived bubble of optimism inevitably burst. The deep, dark fear set in, and I was plagued by worry and uncertainty. It felt too good to be true, and I couldn't quite wrap my head around the fact that this time the outcome could be different. I knew too much now. I was too educated, my confidence in my body to do what comes naturally had been repeatedly tainted, and all I could think about was how much my traitorous immune system wanted to destroy the precious, defenceless life inside of me. I visualised the baby as Pac-Man, being chased around by the morbid Japanese ghosts, and I prayed to my guardian angels to protect it from their relentless pursuits. My only reprieve was my IVIG and Intralipid transfusion sessions. When my body was being intravenously pumped full of those immune blockers, I would close my eyes and envision those ghosts as toast, believing my little baby Pac-Man would now be safe for a few more days.

The first scan at seven weeks was amazing, seeing that little heartbeat for the first time, and coming to the undeniable visual realisation I had a baby growing inside of me. It was just, wow! We were in awe, and I recall telling Rich to pinch me to make sure I wasn't dreaming. I was still terrified, but I'd never come this far before, so I allowed myself to relax ever so slightly. Then just one week later my hopes were shattered again when I started spotting at work. The sense of dread was indescribable, and as I raced home from work, my hands shook uncontrollably as I gripped the steering wheel. I knew another miscarriage after everything we'd been through would suck all the hope from my soul, and again I contemplated hanging up my baby boots permanently. Did I really want to keep doing this to myself? I just couldn't bear it any longer.

I was booked in for a scan later that afternoon, and by the time I arrived at my appointment the brown spotting had turned into full-scale bleeding, so I'd pretty much conceded defeat. I'd been down this road before and this was exactly how it happened then, so why should the outcome be any different this time? The sonographer seemed kind, and I felt bad for her as I got up on the examination table and started to blubber. She must have to tolerate this heartbreak every day, I thought. What a shitty job. I was utterly lost for words when she smiled and told me the baby was still there, and that its heartbeat was strong! It was also measuring one day ahead of schedule. Whatttttttttttttttttttttt?

She told me that bleeding in early pregnancy is common, especially during the first trimester, and that providing the baby had a strong heartbeat, everything would likely be fine. Dr Nick's office was across the hall, so I went straight there after the scan and he was also so reassuring. He did, however, recommend two weeks of couch rest to ensure I took it very easy, and I was thankful for a legitimate excuse to hide in my pyjamas and collect my thoughts for a few weeks. My boss was again very understanding, and I felt so grateful to have such a cool and flexible job that I could effectively perform from my lounge room.

Those couple of weeks at home were a godsend. There were no more bleeding incidents, and I had an opportunity to slow it down, take stock and be really kind to myself. Never in my life had I had a two-week lock in at home, and it turned out to be the perfect antidote to my anxiety. It was winter, so I spent the days in my Ugg boots by the heater snuggled up to Bella, still working, but in a way less manic state. With every day that passed, I knew that the chance of miscarriage was reducing, and Dr Nick increased the frequency of my IVIG and upped my steroid dosage to further protect the baby from my treacherous immune system. I also had a couple of extra scans just for peace of mind and by the time I went back to work, I was 10 weeks along and starting to notice a hint of a baby bump. That felt so amazing!

[19]
Girl, Boy, Girl?

On the day of our 13-week scan, Rich and I were brimming with anticipation and excitement. The ultrasound was at Epworth in Richmond, so we both took the morning off work. We drove there in complete silence, each quietly wrapping our heads around the enormity of our current reality. This was absolutely happening now, and providing the baby had all the right parts in all the right places, we would be leaving today in the safe zone, with all systems go. It was almost more than I could fathom. D-day had finally arrived.

I wasn't suffering from my usual pre-ultrasound terror, just happy butterflies, which was a refreshing change, and as I climbed up on the table, it felt like all the heartache, disappointment and desperation I'd experienced getting to this point just sort of melted away. It was such a surreal, dreamlike experience, and we both shed a tear as we watched the screen. There was this beautiful, fully formed human being there in front of us, bouncing around and waving its fingers and toes. That was our baby, and in that moment, I knew without question that this child was the one that was always destined to be ours. The journey to get here was no longer the focus, but I knew there and then that I'd do it again in a heartbeat if there was even the slightest chance of living this life-changing moment again. We did it, Rich, we made this child! Not in the conventional way, but we did it, and our little baby was pure perfection.

We pressured the sonographer to tell us whether we were having a boy or a girl. We'd encountered more than enough surprises along this rickety baby road, so we were desperate to know what we were having, and we had zero interest in waiting any longer just for the sake of certainty. She was reluctant, but we were insistent, so she eventually caved and advised that she could tell us with 80-85% certainty. That was good enough for me. I was convinced it was a girl, as I'd been visualising a little girl as our first baby from the day we were married, so when she announced we were very likely having a boy, I was a little taken aback. Hang on, I thought. I wanted a girl – and a boy didn't fit into my plan!

As we walked to the car, my inner voice told me to check myself. Any iota of disappointment I was feeling was not only unwarranted, but also selfish, brattish, ungrateful and just totally outrageous. How many women walk out of that scan devastated because something's wrong with their child? And how freaking long had I been begging the angels for this day to come? I reminded myself that the child that we get is the child that has been destined for us all along, and I quickly swallowed any feelings of disenchantment. I then silently apologised to the beautiful baby boy in my belly and asked for his forgiveness.

The weeks that followed were manic, and as quickly as I'd slowed it down to couch mode, I dialled it right back up again. I was fast-paced in my natural state, so in this state, knowing there was a baby on the way, I was flying. There was so much that had to be done! My first port of call (outside of working full-time and attending countless intravenous immunotherapy sessions at Monash and Epworth Hospitals) was our house. We had purchased the worst house in the best street in McKinnon three years prior, with the sole intention of bulldozing it to make way for two brand new townhouses. At the time, we had hoped we would live in one and sell the other, leaving us with a modest and ever so manageable mortgage. We hadn't banked on a psychotic neighbour, extreme infertility and a new business that was yet to hit its strides three years on, so we were now $200,000 further in debt than when we started, without any firm or immediate plans to build and release some of that spiralling liability.

After having our initial plans thrown out by council due to a technicality driven by our next-door neighbour (who also happened to be a town planner—just our luck), we had decided to live in the old house on the block and step away from the project—briefly. What was originally supposed to be just a few months turned into a few years, and every time I raised the subject with Rich, he said it wasn't the right time to be embarking on a building project. He was totally right, but there was never going to be a right time, and we had now run out of time, so when I broached the topic again with him, I wasn't taking no for an answer.

The existing house was tiny, and we had bought it without even looking inside since it was tenanted at the time and it was supposed to be demolished upon settlement. We had never intended to live in it, and I had no intention of bringing a baby home to that space. Yes, it was cosy, and it had served us well, but there was nowhere to put a baby, and we were already bursting at the seams. Also, we were deeply in debt, and we would soon be going down to one sporadic small-business income. We simply couldn't afford not to act now—no bank would consider us for a building loan once I went on maternity leave and we no longer had a dual income. And so, we agreed to embark on two of the most epic projects of our lives in unison. Parenthood and property development.

Unfortunately, getting the building loan wasn't as straight forward as I had hoped. Even with one steady income, most banks wouldn't touch us, and the only loan we were able to secure through a mortgage broker was loaded with nasty fees and exorbitant trailing commissions, so we couldn't rationally commit to that. We needed one million dollars on top of our current mortgage to complete the project, and there was no way we could meet the ongoing interest payments that we would accrue throughout the 16-month build. We could only pay that once we completed and sold the townhouse next door. We weren't very appealing as clients, and even back then the banks had their risk limits.

Lucky for us, I'd established a loyal friendship with my real estate agent, Peter Sinclair, over the years, and when he got wind that a family down the road was looking for a townhouse in the area, he immediately thought of me. The family in question wanted to buy off the plan, were familiar with our builders' work, and loved our street. So, by the time we met with our delightful would-be neighbours, Steve and Fiona, we were already well on the way to making a sale. Selling off the plan is never one's first choice, but in our case, with a baby on the way, I was desperate for some security and some surety to curb my intense anxiety. I felt like I was suffocating, spiralling out of control and on the brink of financial ruin. Things weren't that dire of course, but being pregnant and living under crippling financial stress is far from ideal, and I knew that if we could secure a sale prior to commencement, our bank would certainly offer us the loan. We settled on a sale figure that was fair and appropriate for that time, but, as we expected, by the time the build was completed each townhouse's value had increased significantly. Regardless, we had no regrets. We knew we had scored the most incredible neighbours that immediately felt like family, and we were thrilled by the prospect of sharing a dividing wall with them.

Shortly after the sale contract was signed with the Kerr's, we went for our 20-week ultrasound and, what do you know, it turned out were having a girl after all! It took me a while to get my head around this after fully embracing our little boy, but ultimately it felt right, and we decided we would name her Emilia Rose. I talked to her every day from then on, and I begged her not to leave me.

[20]
Freight Train

By December we were confident we had all our ducks in a row. We were ready to bulldoze our house. There was just one small lingering issue, being where in the hell were we going to live for the next 16 months? A rental was the most obvious and appealing option, but with our finances in tatters, we were seriously considering the possibility of moving in with my mother-in-law, who resided in a small two-bedroom flat. Hardly ideal given we would be bringing a noisy newborn and a 30kg dog to the party! My dad and Amanda had the space for us, but they rightly felt that all of us cohabitating for such a long period could potentially damage our relationship with them, and Bella was also a deal breaker. At the time I was deeply disappointed by this, but I also understood and appreciated their view.

I'm a strong believer in the universe delivering, and this increasingly stressful conundrum was no exception. Just when things were really starting to get desperate, my dad and Amanda offered a surprising and very generous solution. They had recently purchased a dilapidated shop, apartment and office space nearby beside a train station. The building in its current state was uninhabitable, and they had to apply and be granted permits from the council before they could commence the necessary renovations. This would likely take 12 months, and in the meantime the building would be sitting vacant. Dad and Amanda offered it to us rent-free until our house was complete, and while I had never seen inside the building, a free roof over our heads sounded pretty damn amazing!

Time was of the essence with Emilia due in three weeks, so we moved quickly. Our house was packed up before I even had the opportunity to thoroughly inspect our new abode. I knew it wouldn't be perfect, but it was a means to an end and I felt grateful for the opportunity. Beggars can't be choosers, right? Besides, Rich had inspected it and he didn't seem to think it was that bad, or so he said.

The day we started moving was the first time I'd get a proper look, and nothing could have prepared me for the shock that ensued. The reality of our situation suddenly hit me like a ton of bricks. We were moving into a derelict building with nothing but a noisy laneway and some flimsy commercial louvre windows between us and the train station. When the freight trains came through, the noise was deafening. The building shook, and it felt like the train (only several meters away) was coming through the walls. There was no fully functional heating or air conditioning in the main upstairs living space, nor was there a kitchen. The building reeked of cigarette smoke, and not the kind of stench that could be aired away. The thick and sickening odour was entrenched in every yellow stained wall and floorboard downstairs, care of the previous chain-smoking Russian tenant that had lived there for over ten years. The space was filthy, derelict and cluttered with rubbish and debris. It was a dust filled hovel of disarray and I couldn't believe we were going to be bringing a newborn into this environment. It wasn't that I was ungrateful. On the contrary, my parents had thrown us a lifeline, and it was our choice to grab it. It just wasn't a place fit for a baby in my mind, and in my delicate state I was mentally ill-equipped to deal with that notion. I began sobbing uncontrollably, and I was utterly overcome by a sudden rush of menacing fear, insecurity and panic.

Towards the end of your pregnancy, your mind takes you to unfamiliar places, and existing emotions are intensified ten-fold. I innately craved structure, order, security and peace, and without any of those essential needs being fulfilled, I crumbled. I wanted to feel safe and nurtured, but my life was out of control. Our finances were a mess, our home was a train wreck, I was embarking on the biggest project of my life and having my first baby was just the icing on the elephant cake. This was me, the control freak, at my most vulnerable, and I felt the pressure of the world on my heavily pregnant shoulders. I could literally take no more, and then something amazing happened. For the first time in my life I surrendered, and my husband swooped in and wowed me like never before.

Rich is a strong alpha male by nature, but in the first few years of our marriage my need for control hadn't allowed him much of an opportunity to triumph domestically. He was utterly consumed by his business, and it was essential he gave it most of his time and attention, so we both grew accustomed to me running everything else outside of that. That worked for both of us at the time, but now, for the first time in our relationship, Rich clearly recognised my desperate need to relinquish all control.

He told me not to worry about anything, and he sent me back to our old house to rest. I spent the next two days in bed watching television in our near-empty house while he rallied his friends and family. My mother-in-law, Heather, really stepped up, and they both drove the whole operation. Richard's Aunty Kerryn, Uncle Leigh and best mates all got to work, along with my amazing family and a few random guys off-air tasker who turned out to be exceptionally charming, hard-working refugees. They ripped up the carpet, and they removed walls and plumbing. They scoured and polished the newly exposed floorboards, painted the smoke-stained walls white, scrubbed, dusted, vacuumed and installed an entire Bunnings kitchen. They even ripped the dishwasher out of our old house and installed that! They did about 20 trips from the old house with Dad and Jay's utes, and within 48 hours they were done. It was a stunning transformation, and with our lovely, familiar furniture now in place, the upstairs office space had been transformed into a very liveable, New York-style open plan apartment.

I felt like a lucky recipient on a renovation show, and while our new home wasn't exactly the Taj Mahal, Rich had performed a small miracle, and I had never loved him more. Emilia's room had been freshly painted and decorated, and everything was in its place. I could live here now, and I could feel safe here now. I felt cocooned and protected, and from there, Rich just temporarily took over everything, including the building project. I saw a new side of him that just blew me away, and he delivered all that I needed from him at a time when I had never needed him more. Sometimes in life you just need Prince Charming to swoop in on his horse and rescue you. My husband did that, and I've viewed him through different eyes ever since.

[21]
Behold Behold

ON THE MORNING OF January 24, 2014, our lives dramatically changed forever. We got out of bed, got ourselves ready, suitcase in tow, and it kind of felt like we were heading off for a lovely mini-break. Even while checking in at Monash Private Hospital, it felt very much like we were checking into a hotel. It was all too easy, and extremely surreal. I was having a scheduled caesarean at 9.00 am. This has been decided for numerous reasons, the main one being that Dr Nick refused to deliver our baby any other way. He'd seen too many complications over the years, and he just wanted the baby "safely out and in the cot". After all that we'd been through with Dr Nick there was no way we were going elsewhere, and I trusted him implicitly, so I was totally fine with a safe and planned low-risk caesarean.

Once we were in the system, the admissions nurse advised that they had a full house today and that my room wouldn't be ready until we were out of surgery. Also, there was no temporary bed in maternity, so they put us in a ward with elderly sick people. Undeterred, we saw the funny side, and Rich and I spent our final half hour whispering, laughing and making heartfelt iPhone videos for Emilia to watch in her future. We were both incredibly calm, and I was brimming with love and gratitude for so many reasons. I was so proud of the life we had created together, just two crazy risk takers destined from kindergarten. I was so proud of Rich for standing by me unconditionally, and I was so proud of myself for getting us to this point. I rarely pat myself on the back, but in that moment, I was loving myself quite a lot actually! I even felt like I looked beautiful in my white hospital gown, such was my level of self-love at that time. It was a moment of bliss for both of us that we will never forget. She was finally coming, our miracle baby, and we felt so lucky that she had chosen us.

Once they came and wheeled me into the theatre room, I thought the nerves would set in, but they didn't. Quite the opposite in fact, I was delighted to be meeting all these charming professionals who were there to collectively keep me safe and bring our first baby into the world. I felt a bit like the star of a show actually. Did I mention that I quite like the attention one receives while hospitalised?

I felt a bit uncomfortable while the anaesthetist administered the epidural in my spine, but once he was done I relaxed and we all started to engage in a conversation fit for a cocktail party. Meanwhile Dr Nick got to work, and he delivered our baby in what felt like a nanosecond. I barely knew he'd started before I heard that first incredible cry, and when he held her up and we both saw our daughter, Emilia, for the first time, we were utterly amazed, mesmerised and so, so relieved. She was perfection personified, a wonder in every way possible, and the greatest gift we had ever received.

After Rich cut the cord, Emilia was placed in my arms, but by then everything started to feel a little fuzzy. I remember feeling confused like maybe I was in a bit of shock. They whisked Emilia off to weigh and measure her, and after sewing me up, they whisked me off to recovery. I was cold—freezing actually—and I started to shiver uncontrollably. My teeth were chattering so severely that I felt they might shatter, and I was suddenly panicked. I was surrounded by nurses who continually layered me in blankets, but nothing could warm me up, and then I started to feel like I couldn't breathe. I was choking for air and I was in a state that I can only describe as extreme shock and terror. Upon reflection, I was probably having an anxiety attack, but at the time I thought for sure I was having a heart attack and my life flashed before my eyes. Not my best moment!

Eventually, after a strong morphine injection or something calming of that nature, I began to warm up and calm down. I went from distraught to peaceful in what felt like a minute, and I quickly got back into the swing of enjoying hospital, while also marvelling in the moment. My god, I'd just given birth to a beautiful child, and I knew that right now Rich would likely be in the ward holding Emilia skin to skin, a heart-warming thought that gave me immense comfort. What I didn't know was that they would bring Emilia to me shortly after that to attempt to breastfeed. I wasn't ready, and the unexpectedly awkward and unnatural interlude between my newborn daughter and I was unnerving and bitterly disappointing. I'd taken the importance of breastfeeding so seriously that I had even attended classes, so I wasn't expecting it to be so hard. This was supposed to be the most natural thing in the world, and yet we just couldn't get it together. I wasn't used to failing at tasks that I truly set my mind to, and I was particularly attached to the idea of breastfeeding given the unnatural circumstances of Emilia's conception. I was determined to get this right at all costs, and in hindsight, the all-consuming obsession that ensued (which was wholeheartedly encouraged by the nurses) would get in the way of my ability to bond with my baby.

Those first 48 hours were a whirlwind. We were flooded by eager and excited visitors, and my room resembled an inner-city train station throughout the day. Everyone wanted to come and behold Emilia, our magnificent miracle baby. We had waited so long and gone to such extremes to have her, and our friends and family were incredibly invested, having lived through so many of the excruciating moments with us. It was a time to rejoice, and I felt exceptionally proud to share her with the world.

On the other hand, no one really prepares you for how you're going to feel after having your first baby, and the elation and instant love I was expecting would engulf me was yet to kick in. This strange, beautiful creature who I had nurtured in my belly for nine months was yet to steal my heart, and while I undoubtedly felt some level of love for her, inside something else was going on, and I wasn't faring well at all. There was such a mixture of emotions and feelings at that time, but the ones that were presiding were fear, trepidation and dis-ease. I felt like I had experienced layers of trauma, and I was scared to go home, where I would be all alone with our new baby and my exhausted mind. I wanted my mum to stay with me forever, but I knew she had to go back to Port Macquarie, and it was in that moment that my deferred grieving process for my mother began, almost 20 years after she left Melbourne to pursue a new life with my stepfather, in the middle of nowhere, two aeroplane flights away.

Having my first baby saw my greatest dream realised, but it also felt a bit like a slap in the face. I had to instantaneously transition into a fully-fledged adult, for life. Producing a human being that suddenly depends solely on you for their safety and survival is a lot of pressure, and I'm pretty sure I'm not the only first-time mother to struggle with the overnight transition into parenthood. Emilia was growing on me by the hour, but my body and my mind were working against me. I just needed to block out the inner and outer noise and get some rest. Easier said than done when you've got a baby to feed every three hours, and when the well-meaning nurses were unwittingly sending me into a guilt spin with the constant and relentless pressure to breastfeed at any cost. This was the biggest thing I'd ever done. So, so amazing, but completely overwhelming too.

In traditional Chinese, Korean, Indian and Native American culture, the first month after birth is a period of resting—also referred to as the confinement period—for a new mama. It's combined with a great deal of care, including bed rest, constant attention, herbal baths, massage and eating warming foods—all setting you up for breastfeeding. In the Western world, however, there are no traditions, and while in hospital I was left wondering why postpartum is taken so lightly. I mean, I'd just had a baby cut out of my stomach! Why weren't the nurses coddling me?

[22]
Homecoming Queen

THE DAY WE BROUGHT Emilia home, I was feeling marginally better physically, but still exceptionally fatigued. I was excited to be going home, but also terrified, and a little confused. I was basically riding a crazy and uncontrollable wave of hormones and emotions, typical of most first-time mums, I remember hoping. Rich and I couldn't believe they were going to let us take a baby (albeit our baby) home from the hospital. We literally had no idea what we were doing. When we finally managed to figure out the capsule and got Emilia safely in the car and out of the hospital car park, it was dreamlike. I had arrived at this hospital solo, and now we had a child!

We drove home like pensioners, and when we arrived at our temporary abode on the train line, my mum and my aunty Lynne showed up and I just sat on the front step and howled like I was the newborn baby. I was bobbing around aimlessly in a pretty rough sea of emotions. I didn't know how I was supposed to feel, but I was pretty sure it wasn't how I was feeling. Why wasn't I jumping out of my skin with excitement? I was at odds with myself and I felt uncomfortable with the whole situation. My inability to breastfeed was weighing heavily on my shoulders, and I felt like I had been exposed in a way. Was I a complete failure as a mother?

Also, I felt like a bit of a fraud in general, and I will never know whether they were deep inner fears that arose from having a baby from a donated egg, or whether it was just me coming to the sudden realisation that I had pretty much always lived my life feeling that way. Like a fraud.

I suspect it was a bit of both, but more so the latter. I think for me, having Emilia opened a pandora's box of sorts inside my soul, where every hidden fear that had been hibernating within me just came flooding out all at once like an emotional avalanche. Everything was riding on this. I was solely in charge of nurturing a human being. How could I excel at this when I had never felt good enough? When I felt unworthy, undeserving and incapable? The truth is I had been running from myself on some level my whole life. Never thinking I was good enough, and always striving to be perfect—afraid that if I got something wrong everything would be taken from me because that's what I deserved—to have nothing and no one. I had spent my adolescence and my 20s determined to tick every perfect box and taking everything far too seriously. Suffocating in my own private fear of failure, but always controlling it by ensuring I just didn't fail.

Now I had absolutely been exposed, even if only Emilia and I knew it. I wanted to do right by her so desperately and to be the perfect mum, but this was bigger than just hard work and mind over matter, and the only way I could give this all it deserved was to remove my mask and face myself. When that all comes at you at once, it's not pretty, and I feared if I let myself out, I might never get back behind my perfect, structured, calculated, overachieving, career girl disguise. My people pleasing, fearful, doubtful, playing it safe, desperate to be accepted disguise that was keeping me from being my true self. Did I even know who I was without it? The answer was no, but I didn't know that at the time. I just felt exposed and fraudulent. My inner child was screaming, "You know you can't do this". Guilt. Fear. Guilt. Fear. Guilt. Fear. It was a lot.

I managed to pull it together, however, and in those first few weeks at home, Emilia and I lived in a hazy loop of pumping, bottle feeding, burping, changing and sleeping. After seeing several lactation consultants to no avail, I reluctantly conceded and gave up on breastfeeding Emilia. I had hired a hospital grade breast pump the day we left Monash, and that did the trick for the first four weeks. She consumed nothing but breast milk (aka liquid gold—according to the nurses) and I felt proud of that small but meaningful achievement. After a month of feeling like a repressed milking cow, Emilia slowly transitioned to formula, and I started to see my world in colour again. She and I bonded rapidly, and as the fear and guilt subsided, it made way for a deep and infinite love that rocked my soul and felt limitless.

[23]
LA Fever

ONE YEAR ON…

Emilia's first year had been eventful for all of us. She was all sunshine, but we were living in a world that was otherwise mostly grey. I had started working for Rich when she was just three months old, editing and writing articles and press releases that coincided with the launch of his first book. I enjoyed this work immensely, but I wasn't getting paid, and at that point neither was Rich, so tensions were high. Rich had a clear plan for the business. He knew where he was going and what it would take to get there, but over time as our finances dwindled, I lost faith in what he was doing, and this caused an underlying rift between us.

When Emilia was six months old, I reluctantly took a redundancy from Qantas, a painful but necessary move given they were only able to offer me a full-time position entailing weekly travel if I returned. Rich was so devoted to making his business work at all costs, and I knew one of us had to make a career sacrifice for the sake of our child. Especially a career that involved so much travel. Also, we desperately needed the money, and that 25K redundancy payout helped keep our heads above water. I had chosen my family over my profession—the right choice, but a huge sacrifice for me that I struggled to come to terms with. Motherhood is an irrefutable scratch most women must itch, a box we must tick, and the most important job of our lives, and yet at the time I felt that if it defined me, I may well suffocate. What happened to me? Who am I now? Where is my value in this world? Without my career, what had I become? And why was I the one expected to make this sacrifice?

When Emilia was nine months old, I started working again, but in retail. An incredibly humbling step down for me career-wise, but another necessary sacrifice at that time given the long and unpredictable hours Rich was working. My ego was intensely bruised, and I mourned my old self. I felt pretty sorry for myself actually. At the time I thought I was better than what I was doing – that I was above it. A revelation I'm now ashamed to admit. We were still living in the shop, dealing with continued sleep deprivation due to the night work that was being conducted on the train tracks opposite our bedroom window. On the days when the prolonged jackhammering occurred, we would have to evacuate in the middle of the night. There was no money for a babysitter so no time for us, no money for fun, and every time I had to use the credit card for necessities I felt sick. Tensions explicably continued to simmer.

When Emilia was 14 months old, we finally moved into our new house. This was a wonderful step up for us, but the ugly money cloud continued to darken our lives, and things became so desperate that Rich began working for my brother as a labourer three days per week while still giving forty hours or more to his own business. This was an even greater blow to his ego. I worked nights and weekends, we spent limited time together as a family of three, and my relationship with Rich was now deeply tainted by a growing resentment from both sides—so much so that we started attending counselling just after Emilia turned one. We had spiralled down a rabbit hole and we weren't able to find our way back on our own. People say money doesn't create happiness, but when you don't have any and you can't pay the bills, it's very, very difficult to feel happy.

In general, things seemed rather bleak, but Emilia was a beautiful beacon in a life otherwise filled with turmoil, and I was determined to give her a sibling, whatever the cost. We had previously planned to wait until Emilia turned two to try again, but I no longer wanted to wait that long. Rich was adamant that the timing couldn't be worse, and he was totally right, but I didn't care. I was like a dog with a bone. I badgered Rich until he finally caved, and we borrowed another $10,000 from my dad and Amanda to make the trip. I justified this loan by telling myself that another 10K was a drop in the ocean of what we already owed. It was more pressure that we didn't need, but I was relentless in my pursuit. I was positive it would work now that my body knew how to be pregnant, and Dr Nick agreed. I restarted the IVF process when Emilia was 15 months old, and my mum and George kindly flew to Melbourne to take care of her for the week we would be away. Rich knew he wanted another child, but he wasn't ready for this, and I was too invested and too far into the process to listen to his reasoning, driven solely by the unfounded fear that it was now or never. My husband wanted me to be happy, so he conceded and got onboard despite his reservations. We both should have listened to our intuition, but I'm an eternal optimist, and I told myself that life is so often darkest before the dawn.

I spent my 39th birthday in a hotel Room in Santa Monica while Rich made a day trip to Las Vegas in a last-ditch attempt to partner with a guy that could open endless doors for us professionally. I wasn't happy with myself (now carrying eight extra kilos of post-baby and IVF weight), or my life, but I adored our daughter and I wanted to give her a brother or sister so desperately that I had ignored every sign that this just wasn't the right time. I had been stubborn, selfish and single-minded. A bull at a baby gate! I felt uneasy, I missed my baby girl, and I was saddened by the fact that there was a definite disconnect between Rich and I, that despite our best efforts we were yet to rectify.

The next day, we bickered as we drove to the San Diego Fertility Centre, and when we arrived things went from bad to worse. We had both agreed to transfer just one embryo to eradicate the risk of twins, but when we arrived we were advised that the embryologists had to defrost two embryos since the first one looked questionable and had a low chance of success. Dr Kettel recommended transferring both, but Rich was unwavering, and that troubled me. We had come all this way and I had been through so much already just to get here. Now we had the unexpected opportunity to increase our chance of success, and instead Rich just wanted to discard that opportunity? I felt like it was a sign from the universe and that we had to transfer both embryos for this to work. Rich vehemently disagreed, and we had a very tense conversation that continued right up until Dr Kettel returned to commence the transfer. I felt like I was backed against a wall with nowhere to go. Of course, we couldn't transfer both without unanimous agreement. So, we transferred the one better-looking embryo, and the other was to be destroyed. The mood in the room remained tense throughout the process.

A few days later, Rich and I left LA—earlier than I would have liked. My husband also felt like he had been backed up against a proverbial wall, and he needed to get back to work. We were all business and pressure, yet I was still completely unaware that Rich had reached a point of fever pitch that would wholly explode once I took a pregnancy test that predictably turned out to be negative. He had a complete emotional breakdown, and he left Emilia and I for two days, refusing to even take my calls. It had been the last straw for Rich. He'd been living on a knife's edge for so long, and he just didn't have the mental bandwidth to deal with any more failure or to support me through my foreseeable grief. I had been so caught up in my own laser focussed ambition that I had neglected to see the signs. Now we both needed each other more than ever, but neither of us had the capacity, nor the desire, to support one another—we were both just too caught up in our own pain. Rich feared his greatest career dreams may never be realised, and I feared we may never have another baby. The devastation of an unsuccessful IVF was only exacerbated by the fact that my most cherished relationship was crumbling before my eyes. Emilia was my only solace as I started to consider what life would be like as a single mother. Thank god for my one, beautiful, wondrous child, but how could I ever find happiness living my life without Richard? We had so much to work through, and it was so clear to me now that we needed to repair our relationship before we even considered another baby. I felt like I had fucked up royally with my obstinate insistence. My only hope now was that Rich and I could find our way back to our happy place, and having another child suddenly seemed very low on my scale of priorities.

[24]
A VIP Experience

TWO YEARS ON……

THE DAY EMILIA TURNED two was so joyous! And such a refreshing turnaround from where we were twelve months earlier. Our miracle baby was now a delightful toddler, and we were utterly enamoured by her. We would have been thrilled with any baby, but Emilia was simply remarkable. And while I appreciate that all parents feel that way about their own first born, we firmly believed that in our case it went beyond parental biased. To us, and to my family, she was exceptional. Kind, smart, obedient, loving, witty, independent and unusually empathetic, it was as though the universe had rewarded us exponentially for our efforts, and we wanted to give her the world.

Rich and I had spent eight months focussing on our relationship and our little family, and we were the happiest and most connected we had ever been. We had shelved the baby plans, gone to counselling, done the hard work and developed the tools to successfully resolve conflict and communicate on a deeper level. We were a united, allied, loved-up team again, and it felt amazing to be back in each other's corners.

Rich had also secured a partnership that had provided him with a strong network of business coaches all over the world, thus opening so many doors for his business. He had since been inundated with work, and it was brilliant to see his incredible, unyielding efforts finally paying off. I was so proud of him, and he was in a great place.

I was loving motherhood more than anything, and I was absolutely loving my job. Who knew working in retail would be so fun and so fulfilling! I had built the most beautiful relationships with my colleagues, and I was really enjoying the flexible, social, stress-free work environment. My boss, Mandy, quickly became one of my dearest friends, and my "mummy" job was such a refreshing change from the rigid corporate life I'd always known. It was a perfect, easy escape that allowed me an outlet from the day to day and encouraged me to appreciate my family and my life. I'd even lost six kilos from all the walking at work, so I was feeling good physically for the first time in a few years. There had been a monumentally positive shift in our lives on all levels, so much so that we had mutually decided we were ready to try for a baby again.

I returned to Dr Nick optimistic, but still a little concerned about the fact that our last cycle was a total bust. I had questions. I had already sent an email to Barbara immediately after receiving our negative result, and I wanted a second opinion. The email sent to

Barbara read as follows:

Jun 14th, 2015

Hi Barbara,

I hope you're well. Thanks again for everything while we were over in San Diego.

Unfortunately my blood test has come back negative. Very disappointing, of course. We were so sure this one was going to work.

I've had some time to reflect as I took a few home tests in the lead-up, and I have so many questions I'm hoping to discuss before we jump back into another cycle. I thought I would put them in writing to ensure I don't miss anything.

I feel like there must be a problem with me. When we reviewed our donor BYR's history before making the decision to transfer only one embryo this time, we were so encouraged by the fact that the three women she donated to prior to us all achieved a pregnancy first try, two of which resulted in twins! Then there's me. Five "good good" donor embryos now transferred from BYR (and seven in total) and only one pregnancy. With those odds, I'm now so worried that we are not going to be able to have another child with our remaining embryos, especially since we have now used six of the best quality embryos from this donor.

Here are my questions

- should I have the Beta 3 Integrin Test again to check

if my lining is receptive before we attempt another cycle?

- Is there anything else I can do to explore why it hasn't worked?

- should I invest the money ($3,000) in another IVIG transfusion instead of just Intralipids, given that the one time we tried that I got pregnant with Emilia?

- Is it possible to do anything further with the thawed embryos (for example genetic testing or assisted hatching) that might further increase our chances of success?

- During our successful cycle with Emilia, I did not take Lucrin. Would it be possible to try this again?

- Is there any benefit to trying a natural cycle? I know logistically it could be tricky but I'm open to it and would be willing to schedule a last-minute flight if it increased our chances.

Sorry to bombard you with all of this, Barbara. It's just that the total expenses for us of another cycle will just about break us financially so I want to make sure we have covered every base. Also, and more importantly, there is nothing more in this world we want more than a sibling for Emilia, and now that we have her, we know how high the stakes are.

Thank you again for your wonderful support thus far.

Warm regards, Kristen

Dr Nick agreed that there could be another underlying issue worth exploring, so he sent me off to have some further tests. While waiting on those results, Dr Kettel also had me arrange to take the Beta 3 Integrin Test again (aka world's worst pain) and he agreed that I would try this next cycle without Lucrin. Both doctors advised that a natural cycle was too risky due to it being international, which I accepted, and I started seeing a naturopath. By mid-November, I had received my cycle calendar from Barbara and the wheels were well and truly in motion. We would be in San Diego by late January! I was brimming with excitement and surety. This time it just felt so right. Then, out of the blue, I received a letter from Dr. Nick. This is what it said:

You and your partner have been tested for the DQ Alpha Gene.

You share two DQ Alpha Genes. This would make it virtually impossible to achieve a successful pregnancy.

Virtually impossible? Meaning nearly, more or less, practically, almost surely? I didn't comprehend. These words were so strong and so matter of fact that I was confused, and initially I thought (and hoped) that maybe Dr Nick just meant I would not be able to get pregnant without a donor egg. I mean, how could it be virtually impossible to achieve a successful pregnancy when I'd already achieved one? And I used a donor egg, so why would our matching genetics even matter? And what the fuck are DQ fucking Alpha Genes anyway? So many questions. I had to talk to Nick. I left a message at 11 am, and by the time he returned my call at 6.00 pm, I was a Dr Google expert on all things DQ Alpha, so what he told me came as no surprise.

In a nutshell, sharing two DQ Alpha Genes means you and your partner are a complete DQ Alpha Gene match. DQa "matching" refers to a genotypic "match" between the male and female partners…rather than a "match" between sperm and egg, so the use of a donor egg does not negate the issue or improve our chances of success. The result of this genotypic match is the activation of natural killer cells each time a new embryo is encountered. These NK cells release large amounts of TH-1 cytokines that attack and damage the cells of the embryos "root system". It is the extent of such damage that will determine whether an embryo will immediately "die on the vine" (implantation failure) or "limp along" for some time, only to be aborted a few weeks later. If there is a partial DQ Alpha Gene match, the chance of a successful pregnancy is lowered significantly. When there is a complete DQa match between partners, in association with uterine NK cell activation, the chance of successful pregnancy is very small—in fact, it is virtually impossible. In such cases, many doctors recommend the use of a gestational surrogate or donor sperm (ensuring they do not share DQa similarities with the embryo recipient).

NK cell activation only occurs after repeated exposures to DQa "matching" embryos. This explains why a DQa "matching" embryo that reaches the uterus prior to NK cell activation can and often does implant successfully and then go on to propagate a healthy pregnancy. However, with repeated exposures to DQa "matching" embryos, uterine NK cells will ultimately and inevitably become activated. Such NK cell activity will initially often be limited, allowing early implantation (albeit with a damaged embryo) to proceed for a limited period, only to abort in the first trimester. Ultimately, over time, following repeated and successive exposures to DQa "matching" embryos, NK cell activation will become a permanent feature. Once this happens, uterine NK cell activation will exacerbate to the point that as soon as the embryo reaches the uterus, implantation will be thwarted, and the woman will be considered as being "infertile" when in reality she is experiencing a very early, preclinical miscarriage.

In Emilia's case, Dr Nick believed that my NK cell activation had been effectively kept at bay by the use of IVIG, steroids and Intralipid therapy and that she was one of the lucky cases that had "slipped through the cracks". Now that I'd achieved a successful pregnancy, however, he didn't believe my immune system would allow that to happen again. He said he had never seen a case of a couple with a complete DQa match going on to have a second baby. The NK cells would just be too prevalent. It was a lot to take in, but I felt calm.

I discussed it with Rich and we were on the same page. Despite the dismal prognosis, we still wanted to try one last time. Surprisingly, I was not heartbroken. On the contrary, I felt even more determined. Science isn't everything if there is a determined soul involved, and we both wholeheartedly sensed that there was another little spirit waiting in the wings to join and complete our family. I trusted Dr Nick's diagnosis completely, I just didn't accept it. I was more than a statistic, and if Emilia had slipped through the cracks, then another baby could too. I understood that Nick had never seen it happen before, but there's a first for everything right? This virtually impossible baby may just take a little more effort from me, and possibly a little magic from beyond.

[25]
Gonna get LIT!

ONCE WE HAD MADE up our minds that we would still move forward with the cycle, we met with Nick to discuss our game plan. He believed that the IVIG transfusions combined with the Intralipid therapy had been the game changer that allowed Emilia to develop without coming under attack from my immune system, but this time around we all agreed that we would need more ammunition. Nick had been achieving great success with a controversial new technology called Lymphocyte Immunisation Therapy, or LIT. LIT is a procedure whereby white blood cells from the prospective father are injected into the skin of the prospective mother to prepare the maternal immune system for pregnancy. It's a very technical process, but it would basically help my body and my immune system to familiarise with and therefore recognise Richard's cells when the embryo was transferred. We needed my body to view the embryo as a familiar friend vs foe. The maternal immune system actively makes a decision to tolerate rather than reject a foetus. In my case, without significant intervention, my body would always fiercely reject a foetus inclusive of Richard's biology. However, with LIT, the theory is that the lymphocytes that are collected from the father carry with them a marker that makes the introduction to the immune system a friendly one.

In America, you must cross the border to Mexico for LIT treatment. In Australia, Nick was the only one doing it. In saying that, he was also one of the only ones doing IVIG and Intralipids back then. He was a pioneer alright, but I loved that about him. And we needed him to throw everything at us if we were to have any chance of beating our horrendous odds.

Dr Kettel was sceptical of Nick's theories, but he was also on board with my proposed treatments, so we were to proceed with the IVF calendar as planned, and we would depart Melbourne the day after Emilia's second birthday. I had seven weeks to prepare, and I was going to give this my everything. I remember telling Nick that I would be the first of his patients with a full DQa match to have a second baby. He could see that I meant it, and he told me he would write a paper about me when I did. I walked out of his office holding back tears, but they were warrior tears. I felt like I was going into battle, I and I believed with all my heart that this time I would emerge victorious.

In those seven weeks, I started on an exceptionally high dose of steroids, five times that of what I was on with Emilia. I had the Beta Integrin test (as painful as I remembered) that I shipped to the US via Fed Ex. I commenced bi-weekly IVIG transfusions, bi-weekly Intralipid transfusions, blood thinning injections and a slew of medications. I also eliminated all inflammatory foods from my diet, particularly gluten, and I began to meditate. I reached out to my ancestors and my guardian angels, and I started speaking to my nanna (who passed in 2013) every day. This time around, I wanted to tap into my spiritual side, and I believed I needed all the help I could get from the other side to help guide our little baby's soul to us. Something deep and soulful had awoken within me, and I sensed that the best way for me to overcome our virtual impossibilities was to start communicating with my spirit baby, and the familial angels around us.

The LIT was next level technology. Rich had his blood taken in the morning, it was taken to a lab, spun to separate the white blood cells, then returned to Dr Nick who in turn injected those cells into my forearm in the afternoon. It was a precisely timed procedure, and I thought nothing of it since I was already giving myself daily blood thinning injections and having frequent blood tests and transfusions. Needles didn't faze me in the slightest. This, however, was something else, and the pain I experienced made the Beta Integrin scrape seem like a cakewalk. Amanda was waiting outside Nick's office and she said my screams just about cleared the waiting room. Within moments, blisters began to form on and around the injection site. I wanted to vomit, and I almost passed out. Nick was very matter of fact about it and explained that "it's just better if you don't know what's coming, darling". I was yet again reminded of the fact that I certainly wasn't paying him for his bedside manner, and I left his rooms completely traumatised by the experience.

Two more incredibly painful and costly LIT sessions would follow, along with several IVIG and Intralipid transfusions and a much-needed iron transfusion.

I visited my naturopath weekly, and I was able to eradicate the dermatitis I'd been living with for ten years solely through diet and supplements. It turns out I had a pretty severe undiagnosed gluten intolerance which had been the root cause of a lot of inflammation in my body. I practised frequent visualisation, positive affirmations and daily meditation. I had transformed my inner self, and I was ready.

We locked in our date of departure for January 25, 2016. This would be the day after Emilia's second birthday, and more than anything we were hoping to give her the ultimate belated birthday gift—a sibling. At the end of the day, we were doing this for her more than for ourselves. Of course we wanted more than one child, but with the odds so against us and the stakes so high, it didn't really make sense to keep going, if not for her.

I didn't ever want Emilia to feel alone in this world the way I so often did growing up. Yes, I had a brother, but we were four years apart and we had completely different interests, and our cousins all lived hours away. I felt very isolated at times, and I used to long for a sister. Also, I was very committed to the idea of Emilia needing someone else who shared her unique story. She couldn't be the only one in our family to be conceived via an egg donor. I didn't ever want her to feel different, lonely or inimitable, and I wanted her to have a sibling with a full familial link to her.

I took the final week before the trip off work to focus solely on myself. Massage, acupuncture, R&R, and a drug and hormone schedule that needed its own full-time administrator. Mum and

George flew down again to take care of Emilia in our absence, and it was fabulous to have the whole family together for Emilia's birthday. We took her on her first pony ride, and we had a big family party at home. It truly was the most joyous day, and we couldn't stop commenting on how lucky we were. Life was finally amazing, perfect in fact. And yet tomorrow we would embark on another epic journey to sail close to the wind and tempt fate. The infinite lengths one will go to for love are just astounding.

[26]
The Meltdown

THE NEXT MORNING EVERYTHING went very smoothly. Emilia eagerly waved us goodbye and I realised it was highly unlikely she would be in any way distressed by our absence. On the contrary, she was thrilled to be with her grandparents where she was such a cherished novelty, and we were forgotten before we'd even left our street. We got to the airport early and we were instantly issued with confirmed premium economy seats, with a chance for an upgrade to first. Winning! The seats we'd been given weren't together, but the flight was quite full and when you travel as staff, you're not in any position to negotiate. Just getting a confirmed seat was the main goal. I didn't care so much about the upgrade, but I really wanted to be seated beside Rich, so I tried my best to manifest first-class.

As we were queuing to get on the plane, I had a memorable phone conversation with my best friend Clea. She had discovered she was pregnant just before Christmas, and she was about to go and have her first scan. Initially she had been reluctant to even tell me she was pregnant, despite my many hints (not drinking during the festive season is always a dead giveaway)! When I finally coaxed it out of her, she was almost apologetic since the pregnancy was a happy and unexpected accident and her firstborn was only seven months old. This is a position many women must find themselves in since one in six of us struggle with infertility, and on some level, I think Clea felt bad that it had happened so easily for her when I had to struggle so much. I loved that she was so empathetic and caring, but I felt so confident despite our woeful odds, and I was just excited by the prospect of us being pregnant together. Clea had been my best friend in the world from the age of eight, and we were more like sisters, so the idea of us having children together just felt so perfectly apt. She promised to text me straight after her scan, and I looked forward to receiving the happy news that her baby was fine as soon as we landed.

Once we got to the front of the line, we were advised that there would be no upgrade, so Rich and I dispersed to different ends of the plane. I felt a little sad and insecure about the prospect of being separated for the next 15 hours, but I passed the time reading my book titled *'Anything is Possible'*, and I focussed on closing my eyes and visualising our baby's soul being guided to us. I was feeling totally centred and relaxed when the unthinkable happened, and I jolted back to cold reality with the most horrific sense of dread. I couldn't recall taking my estrogen pills for the past three or four days, and it was a sickeningly dark and looming realisation that made my heart sink with fear. There were so many pills to take and injections that needed to be perfectly timed, and I kept the estrogen separate as I had to take several tablets three times each day. I couldn't definitively say that I hadn't been taking them, but the fact that I couldn't remember was a huge red flag, and in that moment the enormity of what I'd potentially done (or hadn't done) was more than I could take. In my heightened emotional state, I convinced myself that this was, hands down, the most monumental fuck up of my life. The fact that I was currently 35,000 feet over the Pacific Ocean and unable to call anyone or even google my blunder just intensified my levels of panic and terror.

I started to cry, and it didn't take long for me to work myself into such a state that I couldn't maintain silent tears. I was flat out bawling, and the poor guy next to me looked about as uncomfortable as a cow on ice. I had no idea where Rich was seated, so I stood up and went hunting for a flight attendant, and thankfully I found one who was exceptionally understanding. I explained that I needed to find my husband and that it was a medical emergency! Clearly, he recognised my fragility and also wanted to avoid a scene no doubt, so he took me up to the first-class lounge and promised he'd be right back with Rich. By the time Rich arrived, my anxiety had skyrocketed, and I could barely breathe. I was now 100% convinced that I hadn't taken the estrogen, and the rhetoric in my head was scathing. I was sure it was all over. I had destroyed our last chance of giving Emilia a sibling, and I would have to live with that guilt for the rest of my life.

Thankfully, Rich wasn't buying into my catastrophic tale, and just his presence had an instant, calming effect on me. He ordered us both a red wine while I blubbered away, and Rich dissected the reality of my situation logically, tactically and without emotion. "If you have, in fact, missed days of estrogen, surely you can just have a blood test when we arrive in LA and up your dosage accordingly before the transfer, right"? Hmmm. He made a good point. The embryo hadn't been transferred yet, so it's probable that the only thing that really mattered was that my levels were on point just prior to that. He held me tight, and my tears slowly made way for laughter. I had a habit of working myself into a lather over things, but I couldn't recall feeling this worked up, EVER! The red wine and Richard's presence worked wonders, and we stayed there in the first-class lounge until I had fully recovered from my epic meltdown. My husband had successfully talked me off a ledge, and the rest of the flight was non-eventful. I sheepishly returned to my seat and tried to avoid all eye contact with my neighbours. Act natural Kristen! I was still experiencing a fairly high level of anxiety, but I was able to compartmentalise my thoughts for the duration of the trip, and I slept deeply for the next six hours.

As soon as we landed, I turned my phone on and I got the sad news that Clea's baby had stopped growing several weeks prior. It was such a stark reminder of the fragility of life, and my heart broke for her and for every woman who has had to endure that sadness. Too many of us have entered an ultrasound room excitedly anticipating that sound of a little heart beating like a galloping horse, only to be met by a deafening silence. And just what do you say to someone you love in that moment? The words evaded me, and I could do nothing to make it right.

I needed to shift my focus back to things within my control right now, so I called Dr Kettel's office and left a message for him to call me back urgently. We were halfway to Laguna when he did, and just as Rich had predicted, my gaffe was not a game changer.

Far from it, in fact—he didn't even want me to alter my estrogen dosage. Clearly, I had overreacted.

Relieved and exhausted from all the emotion and the endless rollercoaster that is life, I felt like I had dodged a fatal bullet. I would never make that mistake again, and I just felt so grateful that we were still in the game. And so it was. Onwards and upwards baby!

[27]
Laguna Forever

AFTER MY CALL WITH Dr. K, I was awash with light and liberation. Our chauffeured ride to Laguna was seamless, and the accommodation we had booked this time was the nicest yet. The Pacific Edge Hotel was just down the road from the Riviera, but more modern (circa 1980s) and quite a bit fancier. Four stars and right on the sand. The Maloneys were moving up in the world! We had booked a room that looked amazing online, but it turned out to be somewhat underwhelming. It had an odd, creepy vibe, and that vibe was only exacerbated by the gush of marijuana smoke that engulfed our room as soon as we opened our balcony doors. Now we were, of course, in California, so marijuana is legal. In LA you are not stigmatised as a lazy, uninspired loser if you use it, but just the smell of it made me feel like we were residing in a seedy, trashy drug den. I was shattered. I had visualised myself lying in bed, watching the waves crash and tasting the salty air. This would be our last visit to Laguna in the pursuit of family, and I needed this to be our oasis. Not possible with pot-smoking neighbours—so gross!

Thankfully, Rich donned his knight in shining armour cape, and he flew off to reception to see if he could make things right. I don't know what he said, but moments later we were moving into the second nicest room in the place. The vibe was just right, and the sea air was fresh and dope free. It was perfect, instantly feeling like home, and I knew we had now landed in the right space for magic and miracles to materialise.

Our trip had started beautifully, and I truly felt like we were on holidays. Emilia was safe, happy, and having the best time with my mum and George, and Rich and I were able to relax, reconnect and have fun together. Everything just felt so light and positive, and I was high on the IVF experience for the first time. It didn't make any sense given the extreme statistical challenges we were facing, but I felt so assured. It was as though I had connected with a new dimension of myself, and she had the power to manifest the future. I sensed my nanna's spirit right there with me, and I felt that together we could absolutely make this happen. I had shunned active spirituality in recent years after overdosing on it throughout my childhood and adolescence - courtesy of my mum, the spiritual seeker and the years we spent as active participants in a strict religious sect growing up - so I was surprised that my perceived connection with my higher-self had come so easily.

When I was seven, Mum joined a religious movement called "Sahaja Yoga". We worshipped an Indian woman who claimed to be a divine incarnation of God, and we called her Mother. We meditated daily in the pursuit of a transformative utopian state of mental silence, awareness and self-realisation. Dad thought it was all total woo-woo rubbish and he had no interest in participating, but Jay and I were frequently required to get out of bed prematurely on weekdays to travel up to 40 minutes to an ashram, usually meditating for one hour and then trekking back home to get ready for school. For me, my years in Sahaj exposed me to some of the joys of spirituality and extended family. We had some great experiences, but for the most part it was an arduous and embarrassing thorn in my side that had left a number of lingering scars.

Now, though, here in Laguna, there was this undeniable sense of knowing, and I found myself awakening a dormant part of me I thought I may never revisit. I understand that many people may think this sounds crazy, but there was no question in my mind. I had connected with a higher part of myself, and I felt it with such powerful conviction that it was absolute and indisputable. My negative, infertile, 'what we don't have' mindset had been replaced with 'what we will have', and I was now all about the solution.

On the morning of day three, we hired a car and embarked on the now familiar drive from Laguna to San Diego. The sun was shining, the air was crisp, and the ocean was sparkling. We were so ready, and I couldn't wait to get there. On arrival we were greeted by the same acquainted team that now felt like our international family. Such warmth! Barbara measured my uterine lining and it was an impressive 11mm. Woohoo! Any remaining doubts regarding my estrogen dosage stuff up melted away in that moment. I went next door for my acupuncture, beaming with confidence and love for our baby's spirit, which I felt was already with me. By the time Dr Kettel arrived for the transfer, I was so overwhelmed by the energy around us that I had tears in my eyes. This was it. A defining moment in our lives that we would never forget.

The two embryos we had agreed to transfer had defrosted without incident, and both looked perfect in the photo we were given. The transfer was as smooth as ever, and Dr Kettel was relaxed, chatty and jovial throughout. After the transfer, I realised that regardless of the outcome, this would likely be the last time we would ever visit the San Diego Fertility Centre. Saying goodbye was bittersweet. I felt so enriched by our experiences there, and by the meaningful relationships we had formed with the staff. They had literally gifted us life, with one perfect child at home and another one now potentially on the way. Just the most incredible, world-class team of genuinely invested experts. I would never forget them, or what they had done for our family.

We returned to Laguna mission accomplished, and in keeping with tradition we made our favourite little pilgrimage up the hill to Las Brisas to watch the Pacific sunset over some guacamole and a glass of red. It was even more breathtaking than I remembered and I had never witnessed another view that rivalled it, nor have I since. On the top of that hill, we toasted to our future as we watched the dolphins on the horizon, and we reminisced on how far we had already come. We savoured that moment, and I felt giddy with excitement and optimism for what lay ahead for us. It was simply a waiting game now, and the next 48 hours would be crucial. Once back in the room, I lit my candles, held my crystals tight and spoke to the universe over and over in my head until I fell into a deep and peaceful sleep.

The next day at breakfast I broached the possibility of pursuing a psychic reading at the Chakra Shack. Rich was surprisingly against it this time, perhaps not wanting to risk anything diminishing our steadfast optimism. That made perfect sense to me, but regardless of that risk, I had talked myself into it. I really wanted solid confirmation of what I thought I already knew, so I headed over to the Chakra Shack to see who was working that day. I had decided that if Jen was on, I was meant to see her, and if not, I would welcome the opportunity to see someone new. As it happened, Jen was not working that week, so I chose a woman by the name of LeeAnn Austin, and as soon as we met, I was so glad I had. She radiated such a deeply calming and benevolent energy, and she delivered the most powerful psychic reading and healing session I had ever received. There were three things LeeAnn told me that I will never forget. Firstly, she said that my nanna was present, amongst many of my ancestors, all there to help guide our baby's soul to us. This was without me even mentioning my nanna! Secondly, she said that there was not one, but two baby's souls around me, and that she felt very strongly that both these souls would make it to the birth. Finally, as we were finishing up, she said that my nanna wanted her to tell me that I should take more walks on the beach. That was of great significance, because in my teens Nanna lived with us by the beach, and she would always say exactly that whenever I was sad. "You need to go down to the beach for a walk darling". I was blown away, and I skipped back to the hotel like a giddy child, all remaining doubts now completely absolved. It was an invigorating shift for me, and this time I instinctively felt it would last.

[28]
Double Trouble?

When I relayed to Rich everything LeAnn had said, I could see that he was sceptical, so I encouraged him to go and see LeeAnn himself. I completely understood his cynicism. I mean twins? We had been told that even one baby would be virtually impossible. Nonetheless, I now believed more than ever that we were going to have at least one baby, and I put myself to bed for the rest of the day not leaving anything to chance.

For the remainder of the trip, I took it slow, only leaving our room to go to a restaurant or to walk on the beach. Rich went to see LeeAnn and he was equally wowed by her aura and her uncanny accuracy. Meanwhile I meditated and focussed on the laws of attraction and manifestation. We were in paradise, and for the first time on this baby journey of ours, it truly felt like it. We were living in a blissful bubble in the most beautiful place imaginable and had it not been for Emilia, I could have stayed there forever. This was without a doubt, the best trip we had ever been on together. We just didn't want it to end!

On our final day, I started to feel a dull twinge in my uterus, and by the time we landed in Melbourne I was sure I was experiencing breast tenderness—always my earliest pregnancy indicator. I remember obsessively squishing my boobs every minute or so while we waited for our bags and customs at Melbourne airport. Not a great look in hindsight, but I was beyond caring what others might think of me—I was so desperate for any physical sign from my body that an embryo had taken. Three days later I took a pregnancy test, and just as LeAnn had predicted, I was pregnant! I felt remarkably calm this time. I had the most beautiful daughter, and a fun, stress-free job to return to. I was happy, and life was so much simpler now that I wasn't trying to juggle career stress and financial stress. By the time I took the blood test at two weeks post transfer, I was feeling solid pregnancy symptoms. I'd continued home testing every few days to make sure I was still pregnant (now the norm for me, and for most seasoned IVFers) so it wasn't overly surprising when the HCG test result came back in the normal range. I took the blood test again three days later to be sure things were progressing, and the numbers were again normal. We had passed the first of many hurdles, and it was such an incredible relief.

Sharon, my IVF nurse, advised me that my HCG numbers were currently indicative of only one baby. I was expecting this, and we were more than fine with it. We had transferred 11 embryos over the past few years, producing one child thus far, so the idea of twins was beyond the realms of even my imagination. Besides, I was almost 40. As if I could handle three kids under three! All

I could wish for in life right now was one more healthy, happy little baby to complete our perfect little family, but the work was far from over. According to Dr Nick, almost everyone with our unfortunate genetic match would miscarry around the seven to nine week mark. Again, I was reminded that Nick had never had a patient with a complete DQ Alpha match go on to have a second baby, and again, I had to remind myself that life was so much more than science and numbers. In my heart I know that spirituality is just science we can't yet explain, and that mind and spirit can trump biology, but it was a frightening prospect nonetheless, and I would need to lean heavily on medicine in the coming weeks to help my body and my baby beat the odds.

At seven weeks, we went for our first scan, and I was still feeling remarkably calm. Things had been textbook thus far, and while I didn't recall feeling quite so gaggy and nauseous with Emilia, I knew it was a great sign of a strong and healthy pregnancy. The scan was at Monash, and like always, I superstitiously prayed that I would not be examined in the same room where my first pregnancy was declared a bust on that dreadful day so long ago. Thankfully we were ushered into the room next door, and once I was ready, Rich squeezed my hand and told me that whatever happened, it was our pre-written destiny. I squeezed my eyes closed tightly, too afraid to look, and when the sonographer declared that there were two normal, healthy heart beats, it took a moment to register. Did I just hear that correctly? Two babies? I looked at the screen and sure enough, there they were, two little beating hearts side by side. I was utterly speechless, and I will never, ever forget how I felt in that moment, or the priceless look on Richard's face!

Shock, gratitude, disbelief, vindication and just the most sublime and exhilarating sense of elation. Richard's face said it all, and we laughed so hard in that moment, because what else does one do when presented with news like that? I have zero recollection of the 24 hours that followed, but I'm sure it entailed a lot of phone calls and a lot of shock and surprise from our ever-supportive friends and family. We were having two babies, and the practicalities of how we would manage that were no match for our euphoria at that point. I thanked my nanna and my angels over and over, and there began my daily mantra to the universe. Pleeeeease, pleeeeeease don't take these precious babies away from me.

[29]
Surviving the Avalanche

In the weeks that followed, I dutifully attended my Intralipid, IVIG, LIT and acupuncture appointments, devoting every spare moment to the preservation of my pregnancy. I'd paid for another scan at eight weeks, and I was advised that one of the babies had an exceptionally small sack, and it looked like it was about to burst right out. None the less, I refused to entertain the worst case, and when I returned for another scan at nine weeks, I was reassured and relieved to see that the baby was back on track with size and that things were looking a little roomier in the sack department this week. I was suffering some of the rather unfortunate side effects of long term, high dose steroid use, but I knew that a hairy bloated moon face, mood swings and extreme weight gain were a small and unavoidable price to pay given the grand prize we would be gifted in the end.

Rich went overseas for work around the nine-week mark, and thankfully my mum flew down to keep Emilia and I company.

Everything was ticking along nicely and my spirits were high, until one unforgettable afternoon. I had just arrived home from work and I was sitting on the couch chatting to Mum and Emilia. I stood up to go and get a drink, when a whoosh of liquid suddenly gushed from me, covering my pants, shoes, the couch and the rug. It was blood, about a bucket full. I was numb with shock, but my first instinct was to maintain composure for Emilia, so I spoke calmly and reassured her that "Mummy is fine" as I raced to the bathroom awash with fear. I sat there for about 10 minutes as the blood kept coming, and at that point I knew it was likely all over.

I was dying inside, and poor Mum was in pieces for me, but we continued to hold it together for Millie, and I immediately paged Dr Nick, who told me to collect any blood clots and put them in the fridge for testing. While I didn't believe there was any hope of either baby surviving that avalanche, I still asked Dr Nick whether there was even a small chance of one twin surviving a miscarriage like that? I remember him saying it was unlikely but possible. I reluctantly retrieved two very large clots, and I assumed that these were the two foetuses in their sacks. I couldn't bear to look too closely though, so I couldn't be one hundred percent sure. The whole experience had just been a gruesome, tragic horror show, and I had mentally conceded. No pain, which was surprising, but a nightmare nonetheless. Unfortunately, it was Saturday, and we would have to wait until Monday for an ultrasound. I remember putting Emilia to bed and calling Rich in tears of utter defeat. He was so far away, and I'd never needed him more. I told him I was so done, and he agreed that it was time to draw a line in the sand. I didn't even share the glimmer of hope Nick had offered.

It seemed pointless. We talked about taking Emilia to Thailand in a few weeks to help put all of this behind us, and I remember making peace with our destiny as a family of three during that phone call. We were so blessed to have Emilia and to have each other. Come what may, life was already great, and there would certainly be some benefits to having just the one child.

Sunday was a blur, but I was so grateful to have Mum there. I needed to be nurtured, and I hoped I could just take off my own mum hat and revert to being someone's child for a day or two. We watched movies and I held Millie so close. She was such a gift! I was sad, but I knew I had so much to be grateful for, and by the time Monday came around I was feeling okay. In my mind, the scan was a formality, but we went anyway, and Mum just kept reminding me of how lucky I was to have our one miracle child. I wanted Mum with me for the scan, so we had Emilia in the ultrasound room with us, and I was mentally prepared to see my empty uterus without reacting. I explained to the sonographer what had transpired two days prior, and then we all waited silently while she prepared. I held my breath for what felt like an eternity, and then…OH MY GOD! There they both were, as though nothing had ever happened. Mum looked like she was might faint, and I just about fell off the table. We were stunned, mystified and utterly floored. Nothing made sense, so we just stayed silent and still in that moment, watching those two tiny hearts beating in perfect unison. How could they have possibly survived all of that? It was the most implausibly surreal moment of my life.

We left the hospital in complete amazement, and the second we were outside, I called Rich. He was equally blown away by the news, and we agreed that if these babies could survive that, they were destined to go the distance. It was the best phone call I'd ever made. As it turned out, what had happened to me was called a subchorionic haemorrhage. It occurs when the placenta detaches from the original site of implantation, and it's more common in multiple pregnancies. While it does increase the risk of miscarriage until its resolved, in my case it had completely disappeared by the next scan, and it was pretty much all smooth sailing from then on.

Dr Nick was no longer taking obstetric patients, so I found a fabulous local obstetrician called Dr Mark Petris. He had a lot of experience with twin pregnancies, so I was in great hands, and he was incredibly thorough. I had to have a lot of additional tests due to my age (39 at the time) and the higher risks that occur with a twin pregnancy, but we were thrilled to learn that the babies were perfect and doing everything they needed to within the required time frames. One of the tests that screened for Down syndrome and other chromosomal issues also provided the added benefit of detecting gender, though in our case all my obstetrician could tell me was whether there was one male in there since they were testing for the male hormone. Ideally, I was hoping for one of each, but I had a feeling I'd be having two boys, which scared me. A lot!

Rich was in Thailand at the time at a friend's wedding (which I had opted out of when I found out I was having twins, and again once I found out I hadn't miscarried) so I was solo when I heard the news. I just couldn't quite believe it when Dr Petris told me that there was absolutely no male hormone present, so it took a few minutes for him to convince me of the tests' accuracy. Two more beautiful baby girls—how on earth could we be so blessed? It felt perfect to me, and it really was. Three sisters so close in age to take on the journey of life together. They would always have each other, they would never be alone in life, and they would hopefully never leave me! Rich was by the pool when I called him, and when I told him we were having two more girls, he excused himself and said he'd have to call me back. I felt bad for him being the boy's boy that he was, but he was fine. He just needed to take a minute to absorb the epic news. I don't think he truly believed it until we had the 13-week scan, but, sure enough, two girls were confirmed, and Rich was suddenly fated to be surrounded by women for the rest of his life. Even our dog is a girl!

The remainder of my pregnancy was textbook perfect. Both girls were healthy and active throughout and they showed no signs of early arrival, one of the greatest risks with twins. Thirty-seven weeks was considered full-term, and it's rare that they will allow you to deliver beyond that with two babies, so once I made it to 36 weeks, I was ecstatic. Five days prior to my delivery date, though, the most active baby stopped moving around. Dr Petris sent me to the hospital for a nonstress test where they monitored both babies' hearts, and while the results were normal, I was still uneasy, so we decided to just get them out. We were now having our girls first thing the next morning. My head was in a total spin.

[30]
Welcome, Ladies!

At 9.00 am on Friday, September 16, 2016, our precious middle child, Georgia Rae Maloney, entered the world. Her sister, Charlotte Lee, abruptly followed moments later, arriving in such a spectacular manner that Dr Petris yelled enthusiastically, "Hey, everyone, come and see this, and Richard get your camera"! There were many medical professionals in the room (as is protocol with a twin birth) so I was quite nervous when they all raced over to behold what to me looked alarmingly like an alien. Charlotte was born en caul, or in the veil, meaning she had remained in her embryonic sac. This occurs in fewer than one in 80,000 births, so it's an exceptionally rare event that very few doctors ever get to see. Many cultures consider a caul birth to be good luck, and many also believe that those born a "caulbearer" have supernatural gifts and powers.

Charlotte is unquestionably special. She is also shy, sensitive, elusive, cautious and enigmatic, living in her head a lot of the time. No one in our family truly understands her, but we all agree that she is a gifted soul and a very deep thinker. She is the image of Richard.

Georgia is the opposite of Charlotte in many ways, and can best be described as a livewire, a force and an entertainer. She is gloriously full of energy and spunk, and her main goals in life right now are to have fun and to make others laugh. She is predominantly driven by her heart. Surprisingly, she looks a lot like me!

Emilia, who is technically the firstborn of our triplets (since all embryos came from the same cycle) is the most beautiful, doting big sister, and I still pinch myself daily when I look at her. She shows a level of empathy and emotional intelligence that is far beyond her years, and since the arrival of her sisters she has blossomed into a kind, confident and compassionate leader who is still the light of our lives.

Having twins, and three children under three has been extremely challenging at times, but by no means our greatest challenge. Along the road to family, we learned that you can't have the rainbow without the rain and that the contrasts of life are valuable, enriching and inevitable. This journey has been epic, but so incredibly worthwhile, and it's now very clear to us that our three beautiful girls were always destined to be ours. We feel like the luckiest parents alive, and while our path was filled with potholes and setbacks, we would do it all again in a heartbeat. We could not be prouder of our three exceptional daughters.

In closing, I urge anyone in similar shoes to follow their heart and their instinct, all the while remembering that the universe is a wondrous, magical, serendipitous place, and that whatever we are focussing on, thinking about and talking about in life is what we are perpetuating. I now believe that almost anything is possible and that miracles absolutely can happen. This is, of course, providing you never, never, never give up!

THE END

Epilogue

I wrote this book for my girls first and foremost. I will present it to each of them when they are mature enough to understand it and when the time feels right. In the meantime, we share this little story with them, and we hope that they will always know how deeply they were wanted and dreamed for.

The unique and beautiful story of Emilia, Georgia and Charlotte, and how Mummy and Daddy never, never, never gave up.

Once upon a time there were two very happy people named Kristen and Richard. They had been friends their whole lives, and then one day at Aunty Stacey's wedding, they fell in love. Eventually they too were married.

Kristen and Richard had a beautiful life, with wonderful friends and a fabulous family. They worked hard in their jobs, had lots of fun on the weekends, went on lovely holidays and played with their cheeky dog, Bella.

As the years passed, there was only one thing they wished for in their life that was missing, and that was a family of their own. Kristen and Richard wanted to have a baby. They wished and wished and they asked their angels to help them, but still no baby came.

To have a baby, you first need to bake a baby cake, with one part from the mummy and one part from the daddy, but Mummy's part was broken, so they needed some help!

All mummies have eggs in their tummies that they use to make a baby, but your mummy's eggs weren't working very well, and they did not fit nicely with your daddy's part, and both parts need to fit nicely together to make a baby. This made Mummy very sad, but she wasn't giving up, so she decided she needed to find an egg elsewhere! She looked all over the world to find the perfect one!

So Kristen and Richard (your mummy and daddy) decided to embark on the biggest and most exciting adventure of their lives! They were going to get a new egg even if they had to go to great lengths and travel far, far away. They had to travel all the way to America on a big aeroplane.

Once they arrived in America, a very kind lady gave Mummy some of her eggs, for she had so many, way more than she needed. What a beautiful gift that lady gave us! We felt so very lucky. She is a very special and generous person! Now we could make our baby cake!

To make our baby, we used Mummy's new gifted egg and Daddy's part, called sperm, and we put them together in Mummy's tummy. Then we waited to see if we were going to have a baby.

EPILOGUE

After several attempts and long adventures back and forth to America on the aeroplane, we received the happiest news of our lives: Mummy had a baby in her tummy! Wahoo!

Nine months later, the light of our life, Emilia Rose, was born. Emilia made us smile every day. She was our greatest gift and we love her to the moon and back. Never had a child been so wanted and so loved.

We loved Emilia so much that we decided to try and give her a brother or a sister. We got back on the aeroplane and flew back to Laguna Beach in America where we had more eggs stored in a special freezer from the kind and generous lady. We were so excited to go back to Laguna Beach. It is our favourite place in the world!

It didn't work the first try, but we went back to Laguna to try again, and this time we had the most wonderful surprise: Mummy and Daddy were having twins! Two miracle baby sisters for Millie! Georgia Rae and Charlotte Lee were born. Georgia is so smart and funny, and she looks like Mummy. Charlotte has a very special, kind heart and she looks just like Daddy! Our hearts are now so full, and our family is now complete. We all lived so happily ever after.

Photos and Memories

Jason Brother with Jason Cat.

NEVER, NEVER, NEVER GIVE UP!

Richard delivering my 21st Birthday speech!

Our beautiful Emilia Rose at four months, and on her second birthday, the day before we went back to America for the fifth time.

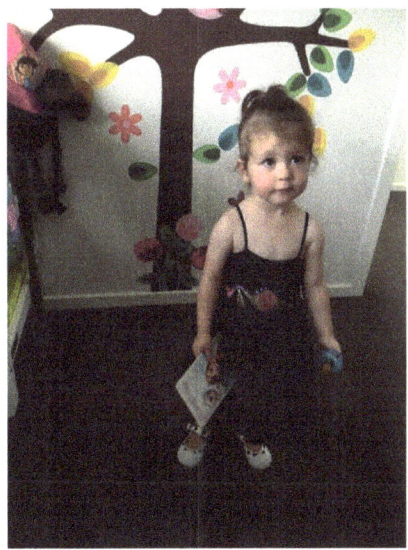

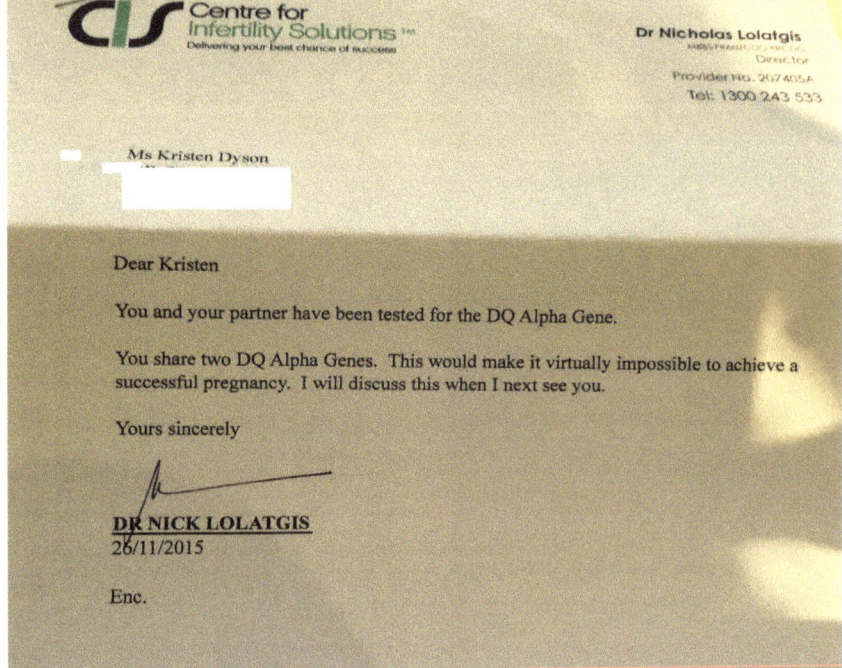

Ms Kristen Dyson

Dear Kristen

You and your partner have been tested for the DQ Alpha Gene.

You share two DQ Alpha Genes. This would make it virtually impossible to achieve a successful pregnancy. I will discuss this when I next see you.

Yours sincerely

DR NICK LOLATGIS
26/11/2015

Enc.

The twins! And the transfusions that kept my immune system at bay.

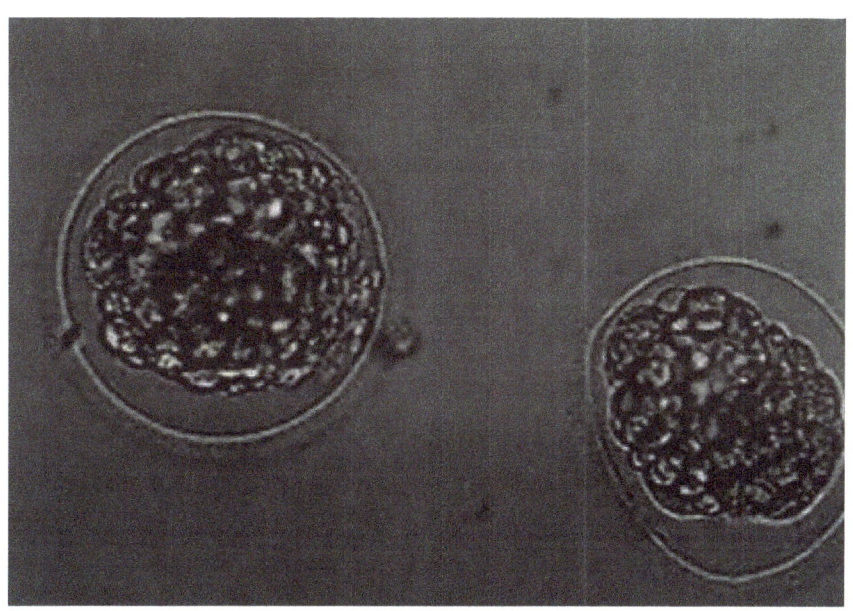

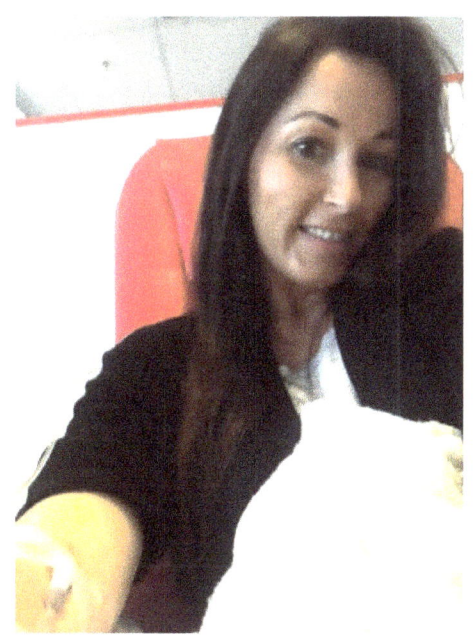

NEVER, NEVER, NEVER GIVE UP!

33 weeks pregnant with the twins!

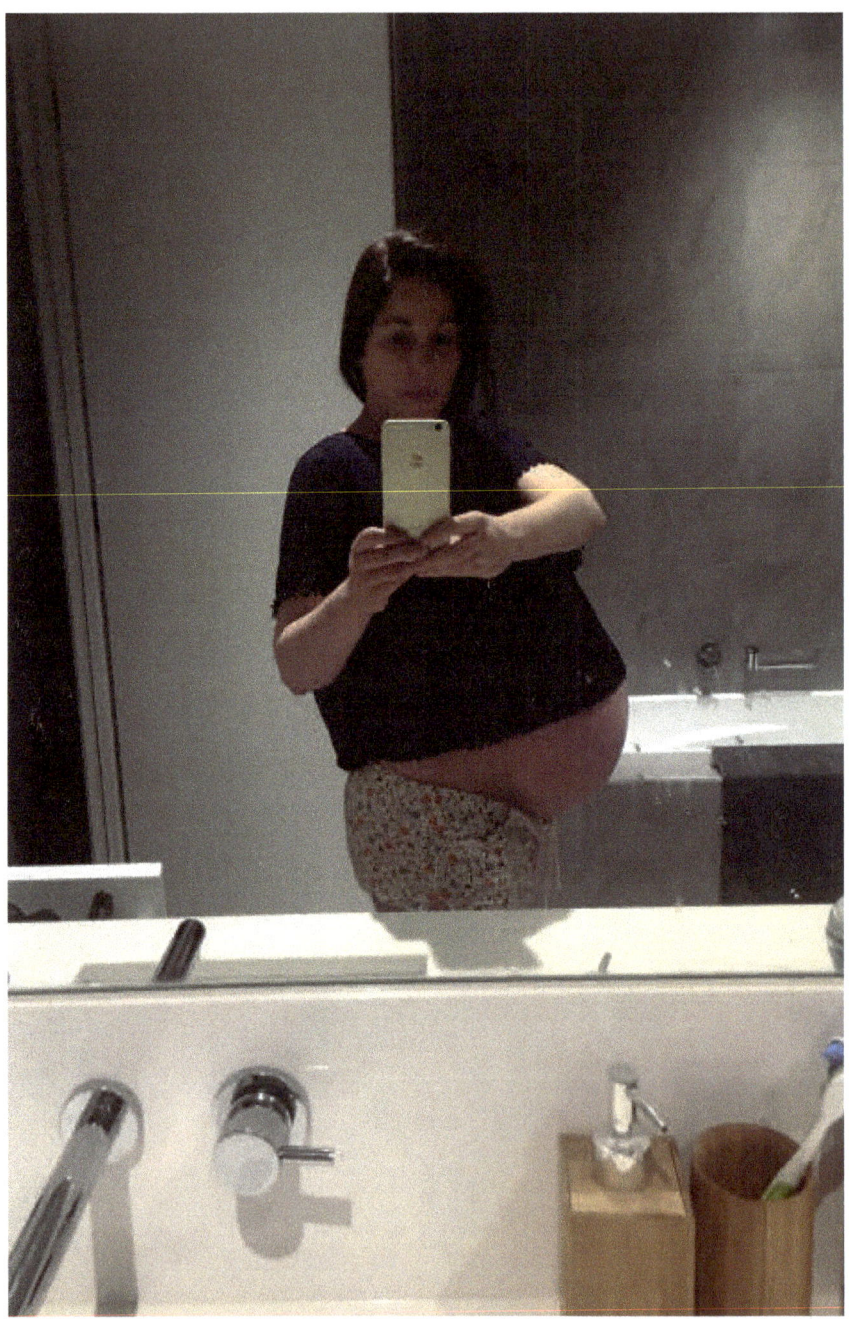

PHOTOS AND MEMORIES

War wounds.

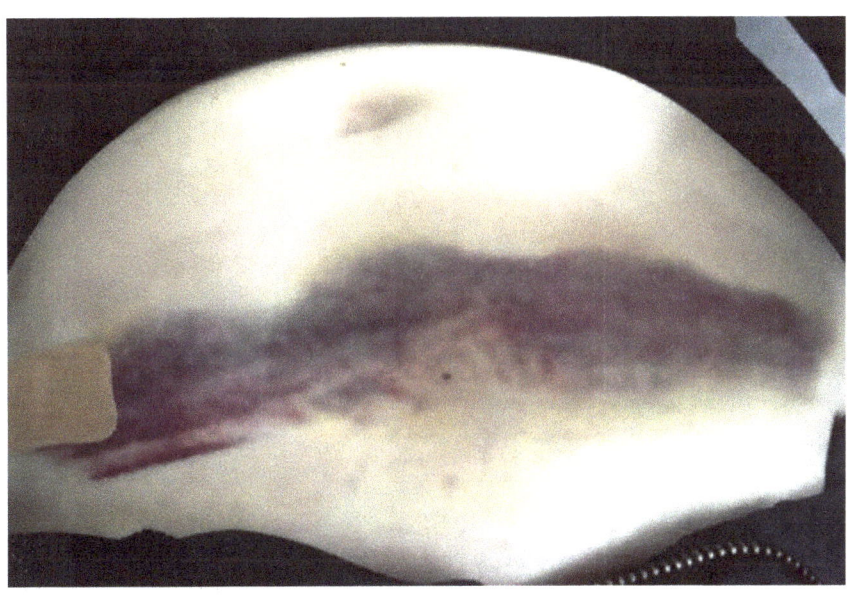

Charlotte being born 'en caul'

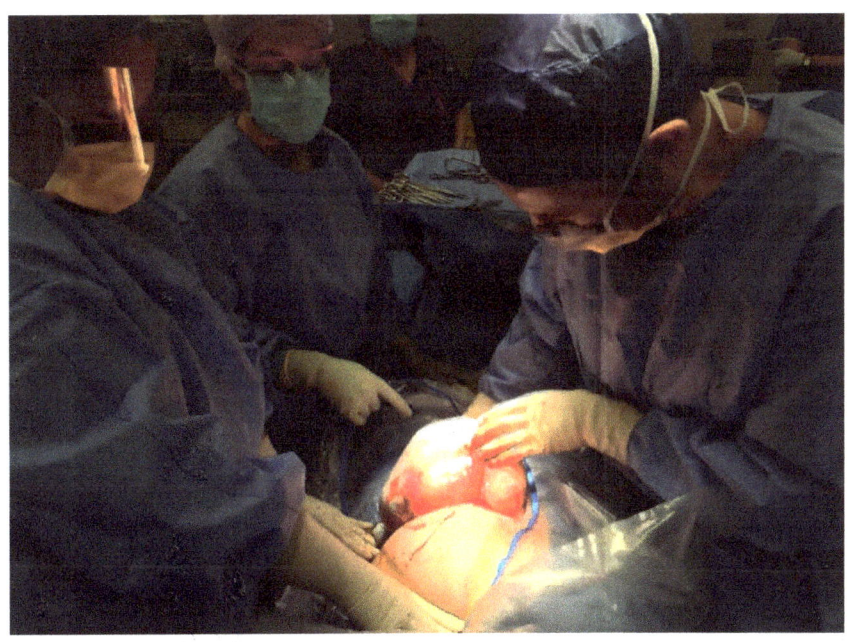

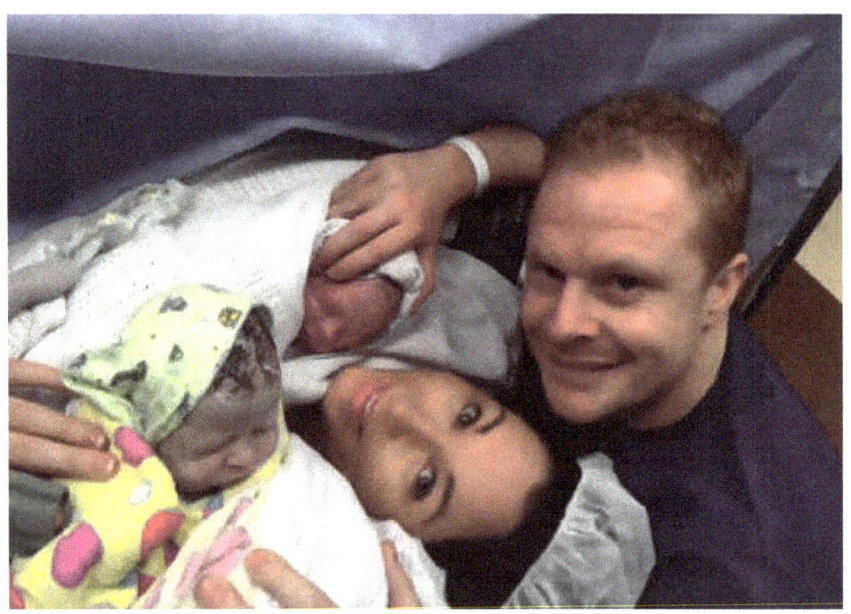

PHOTOS AND MEMORIES

Proud sister!!!!

Present Day.

www.ingramcontent.com/pod-product-compliance
Lightning Source LLC
Chambersburg PA
CBHW062109290426
44110CB00023B/2764